PRIMA
I·C·T HANDE

GW01402646

English

THIS BOOK BELONGS TO MISS DIXON

Phil Poole

Series consultant: Chris Drage

T

Published in 2001 by:
Nelson Thornes Ltd
Delta Place
27 Bath Road
CHELTENHAM
GL53 7TH
United Kingdom

01 02 03 04 05 / 10 9 8 7 6 5 4 3 2 1

A catalogue record for this book is available from the British Library

ISBN 0 7487 6326 0

Page make-up by AMR Ltd

Printed and bound in Spain by GraphyCems

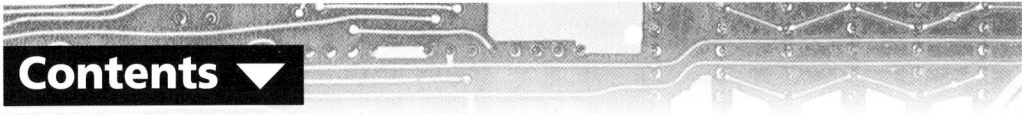

Contents ▼

Introduction ▼

▼ Towards a new definition of literacy

ICT holds a central position within the curriculum because, as well as being a subject in its own right, the technology is a means through which learning can be achieved. As teachers we seek to educate pupils for a life that consists of cash-dispenser monitors, home-shopping, the Internet, as well as an underlying emphasis on the importance of the availability and speed of information and services at the touch of a touchpad, a keyboard or a telephone panel. Not only do pupils have to be able to read, write and communicate through language, they must be able to comprehend, interpret and manipulate the meaning of icons, symbols, language, sounds and interactive texts that are part of ICT literacies.

The concept of 'an interest in books' extends to all kinds of ICT texts: electronic, multimedia, interactive, collaborative and the 'texts' of the Internet which fuse a variety of texts, genre and media. ICT formats, templates and forms provide pupils with access to different genre, formats, presentational aspects and use of sound and images that allow development in writing. For example, the use of an application such as *Microsoft Publisher* (Microsoft) can offer pupils a set of templates in which to construct their work for a particular audience. Through ICT, writing can easily be collaborative, shared, manipulated and passed between pupils, classes and countries through e-mail, text messages, chat and video-conferencing.

The World Wide Web has established a global knowledge economy of information. Pupils' lives are permeated by:

- mobile phones with 'text messaging' facility;
- computer games;
- hand-held digital cameras with accompanying editing and printing facilities;
- home-shopping;
- Internet chatlines;
- websites;
- multimedia texts that exploit sound, images, music and text-based technologies.

Pupils must be equipped with the skills of speaking and listening, reading and writing within the context of ICT: if they are not, they will be unable to communicate and participate in all aspects of 21st century life. ICT challenges traditional definitions of the scope of literacy.

▼ ICT in the English classroom

Word processors, multimedia authoring packages and the Internet provide a wide range of exciting opportunities for pupils to develop their skills in all aspects of English. Word-processing and desktop publishing packages are amongst the most commonly used forms of ICT employed in English.

Reading ▼

Talking books enable young readers to see and hear words in the context of illustrations. Exploring the page with a mouse, pupils can select to hear each word or the whole passage, as well as experiencing the exciting world of sounds and animation that the best talking books offer.

Using many of the ICT resources and educational software will enable pupils to master a full range of reading cues (phonic, graphic, syntactic, contextual) to monitor and self-correct their own reading. Many ICT texts and tasks require pupils to do sifting,

skimming and scanning through texts, as well as reading aloud, receptive, shared and guided reading.

Researching multimedia and Internet resources motivates pupils to read. A range of non-fiction resources such as daily newspapers, journals, commentary, news, books and reference materials are available. The nature of the material on the Internet and the ability to print extracts can encourage pupils to evaluate the texts they read and to use relevant passages to support their opinions. The nature of computer-based information encourages pupils to use search strategies such as skimming, scanning and overall impression to locate information. Structured searches are also facilitated by Internet search engines and key word searches. Databases and electronic dictionaries can be used as a research tool when searching for language influences, or as background material for creative writing.

Writing / composing texts ▼

There are many ways in which ICT can be used for writing or composing texts.

- Through the informed use of word-processing software with spelling checks, pupils will be able to plan, draft, revise and present their own writing. The most up-to-date word-processing software offers a spell checker, thesaurus and sometimes punctuation and grammar checkers operating as pupils write.
- Electronic mail can be used to communicate with pupils from other schools, and the Internet allows pupils to publish widely.
- Partially revealed 'cloze' procedure poems and stories, especially the first chapters of books, can be read closely in small groups and the deep structure brought to life.

- Class e-mail and inter-school links can be used to communicate with readers outside the classroom. Pupils can send published work, or drafts of work in progress, to be edited by another class. Groups can write different scenes to construct a class play.
- Multimedia authoring packages enable pupils to consider how texts are read and written in linear and non-linear forms. Multimedia authoring tools are increasingly enabling pupils to create their own multimedia presentations. Newspaper articles, images, pamphlets and adverts from CD-ROMs and the Internet can be analysed closely and altered through deletion, substitution, cut and pasting and segmenting, leading to the rearrangement of whole paragraphs, reshaping and re-sequencing to alter the meaning and message.
- Texts can be presented for particular purposes and audiences. Non-literary pieces such as recipes, pamphlets, letters, memos and agendas can be created on the computer, encouraging pupils to focus on language, images, form, audience and context. Templates in DTP and word-processing packages enable even young pupils to create professional-looking publications. Persuasive adverts and posters can be created using word-processing, graphics packages and images linked to current books or poetry. Pupils can also write stories and poems, and choose a lettering style and graphic image to link the content and theme to the audience. The word-count facility can be used to help write mini-sagas of exactly 50 words to focus pupils' choice and economy of words.
- Texts can be condensed and expanded to investigate figures of speech, aspects of genre, style, language and presentation. Pupils also have the opportunity to

experiment with a richer use of adverbs and adjectives, altering the gender, style and tone of a narrative, offering different endings and characters, and to use other features of editing.

Searching for, retrieving and processing information ▼

The computer should be used as a tool alongside pen and paper. It encourages new ways of thinking and encourages revision while texts are being created. Scratch pads can be used as tools for reflective thought, with other pupils interacting with and redrafting these texts. One of the prime benefits of word-processing is that it makes the process of drafting and editing attractive and adventurous. Few professional authors work without a computer! Typing up becomes an exercise in reworking the text, adjusting it to the audience and purpose.

CD-ROMs and the Internet can be used for research to access literary works and authors. Pupils can use them to find out more about the characters and associated history of literature. There are websites that relate specifically to the study of English and grammar, and the Internet is also a source of examples of a number of genres and examples of use of language. ICT makes it possible to simulate a busy newsroom, where pupils are required to read, select, condense and represent information from reports sent in by reporters and convert them into radio or front page news.

Standard English and language study ▼

Increasingly, there are flexible learning resources being created to support the

teaching of aspects of grammar. The BBC and some publishers are providing resources free of charge via the Internet.

Assessing speaking and listening ▼

A specific area of concern for teachers of English is the question of the assessment of speaking and listening in lessons that are ICT-based. ICT-based lessons can be group-work lessons and can be assessed as such, or the main channel of the lesson's work is discussed as a whole class at the end of the lesson. Essentially, pupils will respond to ICT texts and work as they will to any other stimulus: through talk.

When not to use ICT? ▼

The following situations are not necessarily suited to the use of ICT:

- simply to copy-type from a written draft;
- when reading longer passages of text, e.g. extracts, novels and stories, which are better read as hard copy, especially for less able readers;
- when using a pen to create text allows for a close, tactile writing process.

▼ ICT in literacy teaching

The National Literacy Strategy describes literacy as 'the ability to read and write', but it also encompasses speaking and listening. It naturally contributes to the National Curriculum for English, but also sets an agenda for the teaching of all subjects. For example, if pupils are entering data into a database, they are using writing skills; and if they are accessing information from a CD-ROM or the Internet, they are reading.

The DfEE defines literacy in terms that include the ability of pupils to:

- understand, use and create a range of non-fiction texts;
- plan, draft, revise and edit their own writing;
- have an interest in words and word meanings, and a growing vocabulary;
- read with enjoyment;
- write with confidence, fluency and understanding.

The DfES has recently introduced a new set of advice and guidelines on using ICT in literacy teaching 'ICT in the Literacy Hour: Whole Class Teaching' which provides advice on how ICT can become a core component of the literacy hour.

The literacy strategy ▼

There are only a few references in the literacy strategy covering the use of ICT. In the primary classroom, ICT offers teachers a range of tools which can contribute to the achievement of literacy objectives. A range of commercial software products is available which can be used as a structured part of literacy hour activities. However, generic packages such as word processors can also be adapted for use by younger pupils using templates, frames and tables.

The literacy hour ▼

A large monitor, or ideally a data projector, will enable the teacher to undertake whole-class teaching of shared reading, shared writing and word, sentence and text level work using the computer screen as an 'electronic whiteboard'. Opportunities for pupils to use ICT will predominantly feature in the twenty minutes of 'group and independent work' time, where many of the activities in this handbook can be undertaken. Unless a network room with 10 or more computers is available, groups of pupils will have to 'rotate' through ICT activities throughout the week alongside non-ICT activities.

Literacy first ▼

The objectives of the lesson in terms of promoting literacy are paramount. With limited time available to cover so much ground within the hour, teachers should be critical users of ICT, only using it when it adds value to the learning experience. If pupils are unfamiliar with a particular piece of software then the session is likely to focus on learning the functions of the software rather than the literacy points.

The objectives in the literacy strategy are set out as three related strands:

- word level work and phonics: spelling and vocabulary;
- sentence level work: grammar and punctuation;
- text level work: comprehension and composition.

Word level ▼

CD-ROM and generic software can be used to enhance word recognition and explore the components of words, e.g. consonants, vowels, phonemes. They can be used in the shared reading and writing session or independently.

- Illustrated CD-ROM dictionaries are commercially available at a modest cost for single users.

- Grammatical terms such as antonyms can be vividly displayed in electronic dictionaries.
- Talking word processors can read back words.
- Handwriting software can enhance the presentation of pupils' writing by producing correct and consistent letter shapes, allowing pupils to bring their visual memory into use effectively to check spellings.
- Spell checkers and the thesaurus function are useful at later developmental stages.
- Observation and memory games can support visual discrimination and phonological awareness.
- Sorting words with suffixes or prefixes or finding spelling patterns for words can be done using the 'tables' function of word processors.
- Wordbanks provided in software by the teacher can be used to check rhyming words using the 'talking' function.

Sentence level ▼

Using a generic word processor or custom software, e.g. *Granada Writer* (Granada Learning) or *Clicker* (Crick Software), the teacher can construct word banks from which pupils can insert words directly into their sentences. It is easy for the teacher to adapt word banks to produce word families according to the needs of the session or task. Once the initial words are typed in, it is relatively simple to edit further banks. Pupils can be encouraged to generate their own word banks by dragging and dropping words from an existing bank as their vocabulary grows. Sequencing and sentence structure can be supported by electronic games.

For pupils who, by virtue of age or ability, find using the keyboard difficult, concept keyboards offer an opportunity to construct sentences from a grid of words compiled on the overlay by the teacher. Images of objects can be interspersed with words to provide a differentiated experience.

Text level ▼

The particular advantage of working with ICT in texts is the ability to return to and refine work over a period of time. The 'provisionality' provided by the software allows revisions to be made without the chore of redrafting it by hand.

- Writing frames made using the 'tables' function can be used by a group of pupils working collaboratively, e.g. planning a story. Printers allow all contributors to have a copy of their work for their files.
- Text can be hidden and revealed by clicking on an icon or pushing a key. Text disclosure programs, such as *Sherlock* (Topologika Software), can offer the teacher the ability to produce cloze exercises or reveal aspects of the text.
- Talking books are very popular, and the best offer a choice of reading level and speed of reading. They can repeat the same section over and over again, and the potential to explore the page more fully provides additional motivation. Talking word processors, which are now fairly common in schools, are useful to encourage pupils to review their work. Custom-designed programs offer a choice of fonts, size, colour and layout, and allow copying, cutting and pasting. *TextEase* (Softease Ltd) has a talking add-on that allows the experienced user to customise the user interface.
- Attractive stories and motivating games, which require reading skills to complete them, are starting to abound on the Internet.

New interactivity tools mean that pupils can make decisions and get instant feedback.

Using information from CD-ROM and Internet sources requires pupils to develop comprehension skills to evaluate and present information at an appropriate text level for the identified audience. Writing for different audiences using the computer can be motivating. For example:

- constructing a web page;
- compiling a multimedia presentation;
- making a rolling presentation for the foyer using a presentation package;
- writing an item for a class database of book reviews.

Pupils can design reports, persuasive texts or instruction sheets and present them in a polished and professional form. Experienced writers can use the word processor to develop the structure of stories, and to draft and redraft their work. Planning layout can be supported using on-screen writing frames. Sizing, colouring and manipulating text and images is a standard feature of word processors. Multimedia authoring allows pupils to construct exciting pages to explore text. Sounds, sampled or provided, graphics, clip art or drawn and animated sequences can all be mixed with a simple suite of tools.

Texts from the Internet and CD-ROMs can be used off-line as examples of particular genre. These can be pasted into a word-processing package for use in shared reading sessions which can be undertaken if a large (17″ at least) monitor or data projector can be used to display texts. Sequencing tasks can be constructed by separating and jumbling words or phrases. 'Text boxes' allow for drag and drop.

Big books ▼

Big books are expensive, so being able to produce your own saves money and allows a greater range of texts to be used. Using a data projector or large monitor enables any text to be shared with the class.

▼ National Curriculum 2000

There are general teaching requirements on inclusion, use of language and use of ICT. A new statutory statement on providing effective learning opportunities for all pupils replaces the current statutory statements on access. The new statement sets out three key principles for inclusion:

- setting suitable learning challenges;
- responding to pupils' diverse learning needs;
- overcoming potential barriers to learning and assessment for individuals and groups of pupils.

Schools need to take action at all levels of curriculum planning to ensure that individual requirements are met. The National Curriculum places the onus on teachers not only to deliver the subject, but also to deliver it in a way that embraces today's technology. ICT is not, and need not be, the province of the specialist teacher. The classroom computer has helped teachers:

- to discover new ways to facilitate the learning process;
- to include areas of learning new to the curriculum;
- perhaps more importantly, to offer access to the curriculum to some pupils whom traditional methods have excluded.

ICT in Early Years education

Many pupils will be confident users of technologies such as video, audio, television, cameras and tape recorders by the time they enter compulsory schooling. The use of a computer, however, usually requires a differentiated programme to develop confidence and familiarity so that all members of the class can access resources independently. The key skills are with the use of the keyboard, control and operation of the mouse and the ability to connect mouse movements with those of the on-screen cursor. Some pupils in Year R/P1 will already be confident in using a computer at home. The teacher will need to ensure that all pupils are taught the correct way to hold a mouse and how to click and eventually 'double-click'.

Developing basic ICT skills

In the early stages, alternative access devices such as a concept keyboards can help provide an early cause and effect connection with the computer. As pupils develop their literacy skills they will need to learn keyboard skills such as the use of the space bar, cursor keys and the mouse. Below are some suggestions for possible activities:

- Use a limited range of software at the beginning.
- Arrange for pupils to work in pairs.
- Use learning support assistants and volunteers to differentiate support.
- Name parts of the computer with labels.
- Take a picture of each pupil using a digital camera and keep a copy on file.
- Many pupils will have heard themselves recorded on audio tape and seen themselves on a video recording. Try to make sure this is an experience every pupil has had.

- Pupils copy their own name from a name card on to the computer with teacher support. Increasingly independently, pupils will be able to find their way around the keys to find the letters of their name. Pupils add their name to their digitised picture and store it.
- Use a Paint program for pupils to 'write' the letters of their name, working towards their whole first name. Pupils should watch their own name being printed, with an adult talking through how the printer is given the command to operate.
- Use a variety of simple software packages, e.g. *My World 3* (Granada Learning), for pupils to practise mouse control skills. Introduce pupils to the games menu and work towards them using the mouse control to select the choice of program themselves.
- Use a concept keyboard overlay for story-making. Words to construct a simple sentence are triggered by the selected picture. Limit the choice initially and always ensure that basic sight vocabulary is used. Stories such as 'The Three Bears' and 'The Three Billy Goats Gruff' are repetitive, and pupils' own compositions can allow them to read back familiar key words, thus gaining confidence.
- Pupils listen to their own words being read back to them on a talking word processor.
- Use simple software to introduce the use of the cursor keys. For example, pupils have to help the postman deliver letters to teddy's friends by moving the postman left, right, up and down.
- Pupils play with a simple floor turtle. Introduce this initially as a small group activity with an adult. The turtle can become the postman's van visiting different numbered or coloured houses.

- Pupils draw a picture which is then digitised and made into a card or a class collage for production.

The use of word-processing software is at the heart of literacy work with ICT. Teachers have researched some of the issues in establishing the skills required to successfully negotiate the software. The use of adult helpers can support those pupils who appear to be behind their peers.

Reading ▼

In their planning, teachers will need to be aware of tasks on the computer in which the pupils are working on their own, and those where they are working alongside an adult. Reading on-screen can help pupils to:

- learn the difference between pictures and text;
- recognise increasingly familiar words of personal importance;
- associate letters and sounds in symbolic relationship;
- examine simple words with patterns, rhymes and rhythms.

Writing ▼

The provisionality and interactivity of ICT can support pupils' writing. Word banks with associated symbols and pictures provide a flexible way of constructing sentences. The 'talking' feature of many word-processing packages allows pupils to review their decisions. With the support of the teacher, a teaching assistant or an older peer acting as a scribe, pupils can:

- develop knowledge of letters of the alphabet;
- use and extend their few known words;
- compose notes, lists, invitations, notices and captions for pictures they draw;
- practise handwriting by copying letters using interactive software;
- compose text with others;
- begin to punctuate and use capitals in familiar sentences.

Planning ▼

With Year R/P1 pupils it is best to plan for frequent short sessions on the computer or floor turtle. A classroom list helps the pupils, as well as the teacher, know who has had a turn and when they can expect their next turn. It is important to monitor time spent at the computer, so quick workers and high achievers do not commandeer the computer. A teacher should ensure full competence and confidence before introducing a new skill, and try to devise lots of different ways to practise a skill. Remember that young pupils can easily become bored and disinterested if the task is too repetitive, difficult or unchallenging.

There are a number of management issues that relate to the successful use of the classroom computer. Good classroom organisation contributes greatly to success with the computer and also helps to minimise technical problems. For some teachers the organisation of the computer into the everyday routine of the classroom presents many difficulties, not least of which is the simple fact that, more often than not, there is only one computer. The following organisational strategies may be worth some consideration:

- Learn how to load, save and print from the program.
- Initially, plan for small, manageable activities.
- Initially, identify small group activities in preference to whole-class sessions.
- Limit the amount of software to just a few programs. The aim is to get to know these well.
- Install the software onto the hard disk first if possible, keeping copies of the floppy disk or CDs as masters.
- Where appropriate, introduce the program to the whole class to ensure a common understanding and starting point.
- Provide some help cards for the program.
- Use classroom support assistants to help pupils at the computer.
- Make a few rules for the class such as:
  - use the help cards;
  - ask at least two other pupils for help before asking the teacher.
- Plan the use of the program as part of a project or topic.
- Plan when the computer will be used and by whom, and how much support will be available.
- Ensure that the computer, printer and chosen program are all working together correctly before the pupils start work.

- Set aside some time to discuss with the pupils what they have done (a whole-class discussion may be a valuable way of developing expertise).
- Encourage pupils to save their work regularly, especially before printing (if the printer does not work it may cause the computer to freeze and the only way to unfreeze the computer is to switch it off, thus losing work).
- Make the focus of the lesson clear at the outset (ideally prime the class in the previous lesson). Introduce new language and vocabulary. Be aware that the pupils may not be familiar with generic terms such as 'multimedia.' If the plan for the lesson includes the use of multimedia it will be necessary to introduce the language and vocabulary connected with multimedia. This would include words such as 'interactive', 'digital', 'import', 'clip art', etc.
- If a new strand of ICT is being introduced, try to discuss the project with the whole class first. This avoids repetition during precious computer time.
- Use pre-prepared charts or prompt sheets showing vocabulary and key functions needed for the lesson.
- Do preparatory work with the pupils before they use the computer, for example collecting data for a database activity or multimedia presentation.
- Give only a few instructions at a time. You may need to give several demonstrations during the lesson. Some pupils will find it difficult to follow mouse movements on the screen: this is a kinaesthetic experience and cannot be acquired by observation. Back up instructions with worksheets or key points on the board.
- Consider differentiation. What will pupils who finish the computer task early do

then? How will you support the slower workers to achieve a satisfactory outcome for them?

▼ Positioning the computer

There is a wide variety of physical arrangements of computers in schools. This ranges from one stand-alone computer in the classroom to several computers in a shared activity area, library or a networked computer room.

▼ Using a networked room

Different layouts for networked computers can mean that pupils may be facing the wall! This will change the way in which the group behaves and responds to the teacher. There may also be a loss of control of the group, who may become unclear as to what the 'classroom rules' now are. These need to be established at the outset. One clear rule is: when the teacher wants to talk, everyone takes their hands off the keyboards and listens. When pupils are using multimedia and the teacher wants the pupils' attention, pupils should all take off their headphones. The teacher needs to insist that these rules are adhered to.

Find the best place to group the class together if lengthy instructions or explanations need to be given. Pupils will become very distracted if the teacher tries to talk to them while they are seated at the computers. Worksheets to reinforce the skills required for a successful outcome will help reduce the constant need for help and reassurance with ICT.

Teachers need to enable all pupils to have access to ICT resources when there are more pupils than computers. They will need to devise a method of recording which pupils have used a particular application on the computer. It is not a good idea to rely on the pupils' memories (or your own!) as this can lead to heated discussion! A spreadsheet print-out with the pupils' names and the titles of the current classroom focus in ICT can be displayed in the classroom near the computer. This can be coloured in after each pupil has had a turn.

▼ Stand-alone computers

The siting of the computer system is of immediate importance. Most classrooms were built before the computer was invented and are frequently not ideal places for computer use. Some considerations follow.

- It is best to make the position as permanent as security will permit, keeping the computer system as far away from the board as possible.
- Ideally, the computer should be placed away from bright light to avoid reflection on the screen. Reflections not only make the screen difficult to read, but also detract from concentration on the work at hand.
- Similarly, it is important that the screen does not face the rest of the class; pupils working at the computer do not then feel that they must protect their work from onlookers and nor, in turn, are the rest of the class distracted.
- Having the computer near the carpet helps when introducing a new program to the whole class, giving them somewhere comfortable to sit as a group.
- Although it is tempting to enclose the computer table with bookshelves and screens, adequate space must be retained for pupils to sit comfortably and for their notebooks, plans, maps, help cards and

other materials. Restricting the space around the computer also makes it very awkward to reload the printer with paper or to do any other technical checking.

- All mains cables should be placed out of the way and it is advisable to use a multipoint socket with its own on/off switch. If you can afford one which isolates the system from the effects of power surge, so much the better. It is wiser to provide sockets for future peripherals like a control box or overlay keyboard.

- As computer use frequently means a group activity, enough space must be available for a group of three or four pupils to sit comfortably around the screen. Younger pupils are far more likely to need extra space for an overlay keyboard.

- In primary schools a computer is often a shared resource or must be moved around the teaching/learning area. A trolley should be chosen with rubber wheels at least 75 mm in diameter, two of which incorporate brakes. The trolley should be able to fit through a standard 650 mm doorway but also conform to the 800 mm depth necessary to comply with the EC VDU directive. To meet these two demands, the worktop must slide out to its working position and be able to retract safely before being moved. For stand-alone systems like multimedia computers in a library or learning resource area, large mobile trolley workstations are more appropriate.

Standard computer furniture will not be appropriate for wheelchair or standing frame users. The answer here is to provide a suitable type of adjustable furniture that can cope with infinite variations in height. Similarly, with the visually impaired or those who have restricted mobility and co-ordination, a variety of input devices may be needed (e.g. switches, overlay keyboard, tracker ball). A larger workstation is called for to accommodate these extra items safely.

▼ Grouping the pupils

Whilst three pupils in a group working at the computer seems a good way of making 10 groups rotate through a limited resource, there is some evidence that pairs are most effective for learning. The make-up of groups may vary and will depend on the nature of the task. Observe the groups from time to time to ensure that all the pupils are sharing the activity and that one or two do not dominate. This is particularly important in the context of supporting pupils with special educational needs.

Activities such as multimedia authoring take time and this can be controlled to some extent by encouraging pupils to create small, successful presentations rather than undertaking a complicated but ultimately unfinished and frustrating project. Collaborative team-work and preparation undertaken away from the computers are important considerations that should be thought about during the initial planning process.

Group structures should be considered carefully to take account of gender issues and equal opportunities for all. A watchful eye should be kept on pupils who try to dominate. Pupils' ICT capability can vary dramatically depending on their access to machines at home. Audit pupils' use of computers at home. You may need to arrange some positive discrimination to bring a few pupils up to speed.

Some useful group strategies for using limited computer resources are:

- In pairs, one pupil completes the activity and then oversees the second pupil. The first pupil returns to their place and the second pupil then oversees a third pupil. This can continue until all of the class have had their turn. This system works particularly well with a worksheet, e.g. finding topic words from a CD-ROM and then entering them into a word processor by cutting and pasting.
- In pairs, working in turns – mixed or equal ability.
- In pairs, working collaboratively – mixed or equal ability.
- On several computers, in pairs, working on different aspects of a class project, e.g. writing a newspaper.
- In small groups of up to four, sharing ideas to solve problems in simulations.
- Short sections of stories, poems or letters can be written directly on the computer. A class poem might be entered and then individual pupils can add verses to it. (It is not a good idea to tie up the one 'good' computer with one pupil entering a very large amount of text for presentation purposes only!)
- A 'computer session' (or a day) for individual pupils can boost confidence. The pupil then undertakes all the curriculum areas of the day on the computer.
- For extended writing, groups of pupils may use ICT for a whole topic while other pupils use pen and paper methods. This will need careful recording in order to cover the whole class.

It is worth considering any other times that you could allow pupils to use the computers, such as lunchtime, break-time and after school. The question of supervision should be considered. Many schools run computer clubs after school. This might have a focus such as a Newspaper Club or an Internet Club.

▼ Time management

The management of time poses most problems by far. It is vital that the teacher is familiar with the software and time must be found for this to happen. This is important so that the teacher may make an estimate of how long each group might need to complete a task. The amount of time a group needs at the computer really depends on the type of software being used. Pupils may need anything from ten minutes to a few hours to complete a piece of work, depending on the type of activity. It is most difficult to assess the time required to complete a given task when using word-processing and desktop publishing (DTP) programs. Initially, pupils might use the word processor for short tasks, such as writing headings and labels for displays, and move on to writing sentences, rather than immediately trying to write a long and complicated story.

▼ Pupils as independent computer users

Independence means responsibility, and pupils should be taught how to:

- handle disks carefully and be responsible for them;
- start and quit the program;
- save and print their work;
- load the printer with paper;
- handle floppy disks and CD-ROMs correctly;
- shut down and switch off the computer;
- share their expertise with other pupils.

▼ Special educational needs

In addition to pupils who are not meeting the NC targets for their age group, most teachers will be working with a number of pupils with

identified special educational needs. Legally, a pupil has special educational needs if he or she has learning difficulties and needs special help. This help is known as special educational provision.

The Code of Practice is a guide for schools and LEAs about the practical help they can give to pupils with special educational needs. It recommends that schools should identify pupils' needs and take action to meet those needs as early as possible, working with parents. The code gives guidance to schools but does not tell them what they must do in every case. National Curriculum 2000 embodies the principles of the code in its general guidance on inclusion and access.

SEN challenges all teachers to widen the scope and range of their teaching strategies. Teachers have to:

- be aware of the range of needs of the pupils they teach;
- be aware of the targets that any pupils with Individual Education Plans (IEPs) have;
- differentiate teaching to take account of needs and targets;
- monitor any progress made (involving the pupil and any available LSA with this).

ICT has the potential to add flexibility in applying required strategies for addressing identified needs for the individual learner. The challenge for the teacher is in making time to consider how these strategies can be applied within the constraints of the classroom and the school.

Where language is a problem, ICT can be used for language development activities:

- symbol or picture enhanced text can bring meaning to print;
- illustrated overlays make writing more accessible using a concept keyboard;
- access to whole words can aid expression and help pupils to organise their ideas;
- graphics can stimulate writing.

Where behaviour is a problem, ICT can:

- be motivating;
- be non-threatening;
- make tasks more manageable;
- provide satisfying outcomes.

With specific learning difficulties, ICT can:

- offer a medium for differentiated activities;
- make writing more accessible;
- make information more accessible;
- enable pupils to practise skills.

Where pupils have physical disabilities, ICT can support written work through:

- communication aids;
- computer access devices – switches, adapted mice, keyguards;
- access utilities and specialised software;
- software with alternative input options;
- word list and word prediction facilities.

For pupils with visual impairment, ICT may help them make the most of their vision by providing:

- large, clear fonts;
- adjustment of colours;
- speech feedback.

ICT resources for SEN ▼

All the types of ICT resources identified throughout this handbook can be useful in the context of SEN. All pupils can benefit from a rich variety of resources that are differentiated to their needs. The teacher has to match the resource to the individual needs of the pupil.

▼ School development with ICT

Without good software, the school computer is about as useful as a cassette recorder without tapes. It is important to regard the computer as a resource to be integrated within the curriculum and not as an object in its own right. Each school needs to create:

- a structure in which computer materials can be used across the curriculum;
- a system whereby staff can communicate their computer experiences to their colleagues;
- and an atmosphere where all teachers understand the possibilities offered by computers to enhance pupils' learning and are willing to 'have a go' themselves. It is only by adopting a positive attitude that teachers will facilitate the success of computing in school.

OFSTED inspection reports highlight some of the problems inherent in the use of ICT. For example:

- ICT is being marginalised due to other pressures and a lack of teacher expertise;
- there is little teaching that will help pupils progress beyond their existing levels of attainment;
- the development and support of pupils' ICT capability depends on the commitment and expertise of too few staff in schools;
- the needs of such staff when teaching and assessing ICT are rarely met.

The reasons for this situation are many. Not least is the problem of technology moving ahead at a faster pace than schools and teachers can cope with. The matter of teacher confidence in ICT is a key issue. For only when teachers are confident users of ICT themselves will the pay-off come for the pupils. Cross-curricular use of ICT will only work when teachers are confident in ICT, where pupils' progress is monitored, and when structures are in place for motivating and effectively co-ordinating delivery.

▼ Tasks, roles and responsibilities

The effective delivery of ICT capability must necessarily be shared with other colleagues, so it is important to ensure that responsibilities are known and understood clearly by all parties.

The role and responsibilities of the ICT co-ordinator are increasingly complex. Although there are many 'standard' areas which all schools will expect to be the responsibility of the ICT co-ordinator, there are others which might belong to the senior management team or the literacy/English co-ordinator.

The literacy/English co-ordinator's role ▼

It is vital that the literacy or English co-ordinator ensures that pupils are given opportunities to develop and apply their information technology capability in their study of language. This requires that:

- literacy is enhanced by appropriate use of ICT;
- ICT skills are enhanced by their application of literacy skills;
- writing and reading is enhanced by ICT;
- pupils are given appropriate opportunities to use ICT;

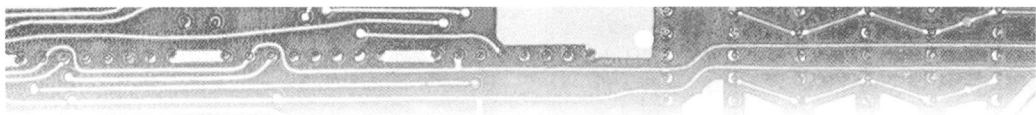

- there should be appropriate progression from being able to use ICT to judging when to use ICT to draft and revise texts.

As information and communication technologies develop further, teachers and pupils need opportunities to use these technologies in appropriate ways to fulfil the aims of the English curriculum. For example, teachers should be able to evaluate the potential of video-conferencing, e-mail communication and Internet access as tools for learning.

More generally, the school should offer support for teachers' attempts to bring ICT into the English curriculum. This requires recognition that ICT facilities are as essential as books and writing materials, and that teachers may require additional training in the effective implementation of ICT in English.

The SENCo's role ▼

Working alongside the literacy co-ordinator, the SENCo can, in relation to ICT:

- clarify the type of help required to meet literacy targets for the pupil age;
- develop Individual Education Plans (IEPs) with clear targets;
- discuss with class teachers the role of particular ICT tools in relation to specific identified needs within an IEP;
- advise on the use of classroom support assistants and volunteers;
- develop an overview of the role of ICT in SEN within the school and disseminate effective practice to the rest of the staff.

Teaching assistants ▼

All teachers who have the support of 'adults other than teachers' in the classroom recognise their important contribution to supporting differentiation. For those teaching assistants (TAs) who are directly supervising statemented pupils it will be necessary to explain how ICT can support the pupil's particular needs. The SENCo may be able to join in the discussions to select the most appropriate ICT resources for the pupil's needs.

For the class as a whole, the class teacher needs to share lesson planning with his or her TA and ideally communicate the role of ICT in delivering lesson objectives. Whilst many TAs are confident with ICT and are happy to supervise groups or individuals working on the computer, they may not share the teacher's understanding of the pedagogy associated with a particular ICT task.

One particular area of concern has been the first half of the literacy hour, where pupils are being taught as a whole class. This can leave TAs without a clear role, thus wasting a valuable resource. During this time they could:

- act as another pair of eyes and ears to prompt, encourage and suggest responses from particular pupils;
- assist with behaviour management;
- further interpret the teacher's questions.

▼ ICT to support professional development with literacy

In addition to using ICT resources with pupils, ICT can support the teacher in a variety of ways. The Government has established the National Grid for Learning (NGfL). This is an organised network of support agencies and resources which is being developed to meet the ICT needs of educational establishments, the workplace and

homes. The NGfL is a resource for teachers where they can find on-line material to support teaching and learning and other resources connected to school improvement. It is essentially a large Internet site providing access to a range of services. Access will remain free and the resource is growing daily. The target is links to a million pages in the next few years. The grid is a very large archive of ideas and information on all curriculum subjects provided by teachers, organisations and commercial providers, and will be available to support professional development. The resources aimed at school teachers in particular are called the *Virtual Teachers Centre (VTC)*. This contains a significant resource called the *Literacy Time* website.

The DfEE Standards Site contains schemes of work for curriculum subjects and over a hundred lesson plans for literacy.

As part of the government initiative to establish NGfL, Local Education Authorities were funded to provide hardware and software for schools. As part of this initiative some funding was provided to develop resources for schools. NGfL content generation has produced a number of excellent resources. Two good examples are:

- In Kent the NGfL programme has produced, amongst other materials to support literacy, the *Sebastian Swan* literacy site: www.kented.org.uk/ngfl. The theme is environmental education, but this provides the backdrop to literacy resources such as talking books.
- In Lancashire, in addition to teachers' resources a resource bank of interactive web materials has been developed, which can be used by pupils throughout the primary age range: www.lancsngfl.ac.uk.

Staff development programmes ▼

Staff development has traditionally relied on resources from a number of different sources. On-line resources provided via the Internet to support curriculum and professional development are a recent development. The NOF (New Opportunities Fund) funded ICT Training Programmes for all teachers have offered professional development through a mixture of face-to-face, paper, CD-ROM and Internet resources. This programme should be providing ideas for the use of ICT in literacy.

▼ Other organisations

There are many web resources that can support the teacher of English. Those listed below are a sample:

British Educational Communications and Technology Agency (BECTa) are a government-funded organisation charged with supporting ICT in education. They oversee the NGfL project and contribute to an understanding through research.

Professional bodies such as The National Association for Teachers of English (NATE) and The National Association of Advisers for Computers in Education (NAACE)

MAPE supports the effective use of ICT in Primary Education. On their website are papers covering many aspects of literacy/English teaching from teachers and academics: www.mape.org.uk.

Educate the Children is a freely available website containing hundreds of lesson plans to support the literacy hour. The site is resourced by a teacher who is sponsored by a number of organisations. It also contains resources for all curriculum subjects, many with useful links to

literacy: www.educate.org.uk. Other useful resources for literacy can be found on sites such as:

- www.teachingideas.co.uk
- www.justforteachers.co.uk
- www.learningalive.co.uk
- www.schoolzone.co.uk

Suppliers and publishers ▼

Increasingly, suppliers of hardware and software are making resources available through the Internet as a marketing strategy. Those who have the biggest stake in selling to the primary sector usually offer free resources associated with their products, for example:

- Granada Learning;
- Sherston Online;
- CrickSoft;
- Broderbund.

Research ▼

For staff working towards further professional qualifications, or simply researching an area of professional practice, there are library catalogues, on-line journals, information gateways and services that give access to archives, official documents and reports.

OFSTED provides a database of school inspection reports. Accessing these reports requires the *Acrobat Reader*.

The Times Educational Supplement (TES) contains a searchable database of articles from previous issues.

Ways Forward with ICT is a report on a research project from the University of Newcastle, funded by the TTA to generate evidence on effective use of ICT. It contains sections on the following:

- presenting texts and supporting writing with ICT in Y2;
- improving reading and spelling with speech feedback in Y2;
- developing writing skills in Y3-4 with palmtop computers;
- teaching the correct use of omissive apostrophes in Y4 using multimedia software;
- reading challenging text with speech and dictionary support in Y4;
- using short rhymes and other texts to enhance reading comprehension in Y4.

The URLs of websites mentioned in the text were accurate at the time of publication. The Nelson Thornes website at www.nelsonthornes.com/primary/icthandbooks provides updated links to these sites, or suitable alternatives as well as a more extensive set of literacy/English links.

▼ Software tools

Word processors ▼

Personal computers are most commonly used for word-processing. It is quite straightforward to learn, and the process involved in producing documents is easy to understand. It is easy to integrate word-processing use into most subject areas. In any context where pupils have to produce written work, they can be asked to produce the same text in a word-processed form. In these cases the text would simply be typed into the computer, stored on a disk and printed out. More advanced uses may be made of word-processing software to create desktop publishing (DTP) products. In these cases the presentation of the text is more complex, e.g. text wraps around the pictures. The use of word-processing packages to prepare documents offers two major advantages for the pupil: improved presentation and provisionality.

Improved presentation can stimulate pupils to improve the quality of the document content. Seeing their own words in a neat, well-presented format can be very enjoyable for pupils who have anxieties about their handwriting. Another important benefit is automatic spelling correction. Although this is not a substitute for personal spelling skills, it can help to improve the confidence of pupils who have anxieties which interfere with their willingness to work on tasks. More able or older pupils can start to think about designing the presentation of documents.

Provisionality is provided by the fact that it is easy to make changes to word-processed documents. This has many advantages in a classroom context. It makes it easier to encourage pupils to check, correct and redraft work, because a rewrite is much less of a chore. At a basic level, this can mean removing obvious errors. Older pupils can start to think about using alternative wording, or rearranging the order of paragraphs. More able pupils can use this feature of word-processing packages to prepare outlines of essays in advance, or to explore the effects of making different changes to text documents.

The main disadvantage of producing text using word-processing is that the pupil is not as free to continue the task outside the classroom, e.g. for homework. It is important to ensure that time and resources are available for the pupils to produce any documentation which is required in word-processed form. It is better for pupils to compose the work as they type, rather than to copy-type from documents they have written by hand, since this can be very boring and can put them off using the computer. It also takes away the advantage of provisionality. Ideally, as pupils become confident in using the computer they should be constantly revising and correcting as they work on the document. Copying a piece of text word-for-word removes this major advantage.

Word-processing does not require advanced equipment. Almost any computer/printer combination can be used to produce word-processed documents, and the software is very widely available. In classrooms where pupils have to share computers, this is not satisfactory for most word-processing tasks. If pupils are using the word processor to compose new documents, as they would when working with pen and paper, then they need to have uninterrupted one-to-one access. There are, however, group tasks that could be carried out in pairs or groups using word-processing software, such as writing letters to request information or producing a class newsletter. It is important to organise 'off-computer' work for pupils, such

as task planning, preparing graphic work, etc. Whatever arrangements are deployed, a printer will allow all contributors to have a copy of their own work.

Word processors also offer other useful tools:

- text boxes;
- text highlighting;
- thesaurus;
- spell checking;
- drag and drop.

For organising and controlling the position of words or text constraining the layout, using the 'tables' function is a powerful tool. Tables are made up of a matrix of rows and columns. The height of a row can be fixed or can grow with the amount of text entered. Mastering the 'tables' function is a must for all teachers at a professional level for making planning tools, or in producing ICT activities.

Writing frames ▼

Scaffolding pupils' story-writing and guiding their research in a non-fiction context can be achieved through the use of writing frames. Using ICT to create frames for pupils to write on or type in can be done in a variety of ways:

- The 'tables' function is a way of creating and controlling the size of boxes containing guidance text.
- Use the 'forms' tool bar, select the frame tool to drag out a box which can hold a predefined number of words in a particular style of text.
- Most word processors have a drawing menu which supports the use of drawn shapes such as rectangles, circles, ellipses.
- *TextEase 2000* (Softease) or *Granada Writer* (Granada Learning) offer the freedom to

place text anywhere on the page and then enclose it with a drawn frame.

The addition of clip art can offer visual clues and produce a more interesting backdrop to the pupils' written ideas. Tutorials on creating frames are available on the software publishers' website.

More sophisticated word-processing software, and software designed specifically for primary work or SEN support, can offer additional important features such as:

- a reduced menu of functions on the toolbar;
- the ability to change the toolbar according to the experience of the pupils;
- words can be inserted anywhere on the page and 'float' over the text;
- a speech facility to 'read back' text;
- simple creating of tables or columns;
- the ability to track changes (trace editing);
- the facility to save work from the web (html files).

Teachers can make use of word-processing to help them with their own work. With the emphasis on whole-class teaching in the literacy hour, word processors can provide resources to support particular teaching points, e.g. highlighting aspects of grammar.

At a planning level, they can be used to generate weekly or termly planning sheets which can be readily edited from year to year. The teacher can create documents for class use, such as handouts and worksheets. With practice, this can be quicker than writing them by hand, and the clarity and quality will generally be higher. If teachers want pupils to produce high quality documentation, then they must lead by example. Teachers can produce outline or template documents, and distribute them in electronic form to the class. If they

want to guide pupils' research or steer the development of ideas for a story, then a writing frame is useful. For pupils who have suitable keyboard skills, teachers can copy this file from their disk (or over the network) to each pupil, who then fill in the gaps. If teachers want to give more help than this, they can provide more of the text, and leave smaller gaps.

Desktop publishing (DTP) ▼

Older word-processing packages simply allowed for plain text documents, set out as a simple typed page. DTP packages such as *Adobe Pagemaker* were an exciting new development, allowing the user to create advanced effects by adding pictures and arranging text on the page like a professional printer. Today, the distinction between these two types of package is less important unless a commercial printer requires an electronic document. Modern word-processing packages include many DTP features. With practice, it is possible to produce almost any kind of document with a word-processing package such as *Granada Writer* (Granada Learning). The latter offers a range of creative templates and tools which support the development of professional-looking products such as leaflets, brochures and newsletters.

Presentation software ▼

Presentation software began as a facility for presentations at conferences and meetings. It produced overhead transparencies, and then with the developments in data projectors it became possible to show the screen directly to the audience, e.g. *TextEase Presenter* (Softease).

Presentation software can be used:

- to produce a series of linear screens with graphics;
- to produce animation effects that teachers can use to highlight particular grammatical elements, word endings, etc.
- templates provided with the package can make a few words look very impressive, and this can be useful to motivate pupils who find writing at length difficult;
- multimedia functions such as graphics, sound and animation can be used to produce talking book-type presentations to promote speaking and listening skills.

Multimedia authoring programs offer more sophisticated media features than presentation software.

Multimedia ▼

Multimedia provides an exciting new way of presenting information in an interactive and non-linear format. Web page design now incorporates multimedia features such as sound and animation. Multimedia is the mixing of different forms of media within one program. Such media may include text, graphics – in the form of drawings, clip art, scanned photographs or images from digital cameras – video clips, sound clips or animations. A number of commercial multimedia programs currently available attempt to stimulate and intrigue pupils. These programs range from the popular talking books which are designed to engage early readers, through to CD-ROM-based reference material. The key to the success of each is often in its level of interactivity, i.e. the way in which the user can, to a greater or lesser extent, determine the order in which the various elements are presented. Increasingly, the Internet is providing multimedia resources to support literacy activities, e.g. *Talking Books*.

Special software, called 'multimedia authoring' packages provide opportunities for

pupils not just to respond to commercial multimedia programs, but also to be able to design and author their own multimedia material for others to use. Presentation packages such as *Microsoft PowerPoint* can be used to author multimedia materials, but have limited features. One of the most popular packages used in primary schools is *Hyperstudio*.

These packages are now sufficiently straightforward and robust for pupils to use with only limited support from the teacher, after a modest induction process. The packages are underpinned by their ability to create and link a series of computer 'screens' which can be linked dynamically through the creation of buttons or 'hotspots'. By clicking on these the user can navigate to another screen, reveal text, hear a sound or play an animation or video. Many packages now have the facility to create buttons which activate web links, opening up the possibility of pupils publishing material directly linked to the Internet. Pupils could create their own talking storybook, a school guide for new pupils or visiting parents, a language-matching exercise, a history quiz … the possibilities are limitless.

Effective work with multimedia authoring requires access to modern computer hardware which includes a sound card and a CD-ROM drive. A scanner and digital camera are also recommended. The files which are created, particularly those using graphics and sound, take up a large amount of computer memory and will not generally fit on a floppy disk.

Planning software ▼

Planning software can support pupils in the planning process for extended writing. The teacher can also use it for teaching shared writing. Software such as *Inspirations* (TAG) enables ideas to be collected and represented on the screen using a number of graphical tools, such as boxes linked as spider diagrams. The creation of writing frames and tables in conventional word-processing software can also support planning. Planning is an important strategy in supporting pupils with dyslexia.

Wordbanks ▼

Software such as *Clicker* (Crick Software) or *Granada Writer* (Granada Learning) enable words to be selected from a bank of words and inserted into a word-processing area of the screen. Word banks can be used across the whole primary age range, and for written work in most subjects where new vocabulary is being introduced. They have been found to be particularly useful in the context of SEN, where they can support word recognition, spelling and sentence construction and help pupils with physical disabilities that make extended use of the keyboard entry difficult. A good word bank programme should:

- provide a simple interface through which teachers can create new banks;
- have pictures which can be associated with a word;
- enable changes in font size and style to be made;
- have a speech facility to read words and sentences;
- allow phrases as well as words to be added.

Spelling and grammar reinforcement programs ▼

Content specific programs are particularly useful in remedial work when pupils are failing to meet their expected targets in these areas. Integrated Learning System (ILS) can identify and track pupils' progress which means they can set tasks appropriate to the level at which the pupil is operating. These can be used for whole-class work within the literacy hour or as part of a remedial programme, or to support SEN provisions. Make purchasing decisions on the extent to which the teacher can easily author the programme and set the level of tasks provided for individuals.

Dictionaries and encyclopedias ▼

Pupils need access to a wide range of texts in different media. The World Wide Web and CD-ROM encyclopedias are useful sources of text which can contain:

- hyperlinks to other media;
- search facilities;
- indexes;
- labels and captions;
- non-fiction text.

The benefits of electronic encyclopedias for rapidly searching for the origins of words or similar grammatical forms can easily be demonstrated. Alternatives to alphabetical scanning of conventional dictionaries encourage pupils to experiment with searching for words. A speaking function can help them check phonically that they have the right word.

E-mail ▼

Writing for a purpose, and for a different audience, is very important for a pupil. The thought that another person, perhaps thousands of miles away, can be sent an electronic 'letter' which can be received in less than a minute is a very powerful experience for most pupils. There are two types of e-mail software:

Web-based mail systems: these are mail services which use software on the Internet itself, e.g. *Yahoo mail* or *WebMail*. They require the user to be logged onto the Internet so charges are incurred during composition of a message. Mailboxes can, however, be accessed on any computer with Internet facilities.

Computer-based mail software: software to access the mailbox is based on the computer which can restrict access from other places if it is not available, e.g. *Microsoft Outlook Express*. Composition can be done off-line which is useful if a class generates a large number of messages which can be queued and then sent in a few seconds when logged onto the Internet.

E-mail messages travel via an 'electronic post office', where they wait until the intended recipient checks if there are any messages. Each user has a unique identification code (i.e. an address) which ensures that users get only the messages intended for them. Not all schools will be able to manage to provide an e-mail address for each pupil, so they may have to share. In school, teachers have found that managing e-mails can be like trying to steer an avalanche!

On-line time costs money, so teach pupils to type messages in Word before going on-line, to store the text and then 'paste' the messages into the mail program. E-mail can be a valuable tool for allowing pupils to communicate with the world at large; it can also be abused, with inappropriate materials being both sent and received. The school's Internet provider will supply the school with at least one e-mail address, but pupils may have been allocated their own addresses already. If there is only one address for a class, pupils will need to identify themselves so that messages reach the right person.

It is important to ensure that pupils follow 'classroom rules' for the use of e-mails. It will probably be necessary to ration the use of the computer for e-mails, perhaps limiting it to one session a week. If you have a 'partner' school, inform them that you are limited in time and access to hardware. Whatever system is used, it is very important that it is fair and ensures that all pupils have equal access. Some considerations are:

- How can the teacher keep track of how many e-mails pupils are sending?
- How will the teacher ensure that the pupils have a similar entitlement for each session? What limits will be imposed (e.g. two paragraphs maximum)?
- How will the content of the messages be monitored?
- Who will have the responsibility for sending the e-mail by dialling out?
- Is the password permanently stored in the computer?
- Can pupils keep copies of their e-mails, either by storing them on the hard drive/floppy disk or printing them out?
- How can higher order language skills be encouraged, rather than simply 'Hello, I am Jack. I live at ...'?

The 'National Grid for Learning' initiative is going to connect all schools to the Internet. Once a school has the necessary e-mail facilities the next stage is to try to set up some links with other local, national and international schools. For the security of the pupils, the teacher should make sure that:

- pupils do not include their age, home address or a telephone number in an e-mail;
- the school fax or telephone number is only quoted in exceptional circumstances;

- permission is obtained from parents before a photograph of the pupil is attached to an e-mail. (Generally avoid photographs.)

Internet ▼

There are good educational reasons for using the Internet, such as undertaking research, obtaining up-to-date news and weather reports, sending and receiving e-mail, using chatlines and forums and publishing web pages. The Internet started as a defence-related network. It has grown into a global network of linked computer networks making a web of connections. The World Wide Web (www) is a network of computers linking thousands of 'sites', and millions of contributors and users. E-mail services are also routed on the Internet as well as telecommunications traffic such as video, audio and other digital resources shared between companies and organisations. Using the facilities of the Internet it is possible for teachers and pupils to:

- access information on almost any subject;
- learn and revise using multimedia teaching and learning materials;
- download software and data files;
- order resources;
- browse library catalogues around the world;
- obtain up-to-date news reports;
- send and receive e-mail;
- communicate with people having similar interests using chatlines and forums;
- publish information for others to see.

Information on the www is organised into 'pages', each one with its own unique address on the network, called a URL (uniform resource locator). The pages are accessed using this address which appears in the 'location' box of the web browser. The address is typed

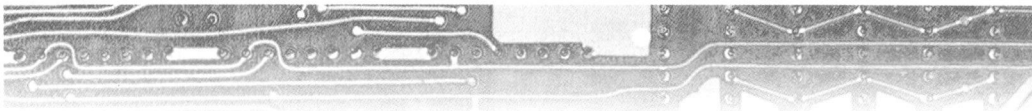

in or can be automatically entered from the 'bookmark' or 'favourite' function of the browser. 'Bookmarking' enables site addresses to be stored, avoiding the necessity for 'browsing' to get to them.

On a web page text, pictures and graphics can be 'hot-linked' to other pages. The links are usually referred to as hypertext links. Jumping from one link to another is called 'browsing'. Pages are created using a programming language, the most commonly used being HTML (hypertext mark-up language). Authoring can be done using a word processor or a special authoring package, e.g. *Site Central* (TAG Learning). Teachers and pupils will increasingly be contributors to the resources of the www. A school can also gain valuable publicity by having its own website!

It is often said that any book containing information is out-of-date as soon as it is published, and the Internet can help overcome this problem. However, there is less control over the content of information appearing on the Internet than in paper-based publications. Anyone can publish information on the Internet, regardless of how little they know about a subject and who they represent. Pupils have to learn to be discerning, selective authors to use the resources effectively.

Before letting a class loose on the Internet, teachers need a strategy that will identify promising material and avoid the more dubious websites. In particular, look for sites that provide useful hot links to other sites. Pupils enjoy surfing productively, but they go off-task quickly if they cannot find relevant information. Learning to use a browser teaches pupils useful search skills. Give some basic starting points (how to type in Internet addresses or URLs and use the 'back' and 'forward' buttons), but let them make their own mistakes. Encourage pupils to keep the

addresses of useful websites for future use. Using a search engine teaches pupils important research techniques. The key to success is learning how to define and refine searches to find exactly what is required.

Teachers need to build up a personal list of useful websites, and amend this as necessary. Bookmarks can be kept on a disk and imported into the browser. Provide pupils with a list of bookmarks to work from, or put the topic links onto a school website page for pupils to download.

▼ Hardware tools

Digital cameras ▼

Digital cameras are now affordable and desirable as schools establish ICT across the school and begin to build websites. When purchasing a digital camera the school should consider:

- price range;
- quality of the image required; images on websites are less demanding than print (generally the higher the quality of the image the greater the memory required for each file);
- ease of transfer of files from camera to computer (cameras that write directly to a floppy disk will be used the most around the school).

Scanners ▼

Scanners are essential for converting pupils' illustrations into an electronic format. Pupils naturally illustrate their written work and this is not always possible on the computer. Clip art is a substitute, but it inevitably restricts choice and is rarely as imaginative as pupils' own work. For under £50 a single scanner can

enable the pupils' illustrations to be placed alongside their written work. The images can take up a considerable amount of memory. However, the scanning software should allow the conversion from a bitmap to a more compressed image format such as *.jpeg* or *.giff* with little loss of quality. Although existing pictures can be scanned, the quality of an image will be inferior to an original image from a digital camera.

Data projectors ▼

Even using a large monitor for whole-class teaching in the literacy hour it can be difficult for the whole group to see clearly. Data projectors provide an image the size of that from an overhead projector on a screen. Good quality projectors produce an image that is bright enough to be seen without blacking out the room. The projector is plugged into the computer instead of the monitor. However, a return loop means that the monitor can be on at the same time. These work just as well with a laptop computer which can create a mobile resource that can be used around the school. This resource, more than any other, can transform the single classroom computer into a whole-class resource. Pupils and the teacher can:

- examine pieces of text or a poem in detail using highlights;
- highlight features of sentences;
- move words, sentences or paragraphs to respond to pupils' suggestions using 'drag and drop' or 'cut and paste' features;
- discuss experiments with vocabulary, fonts or layout;
- use the grammar checker to consider sentence construction;
- read big books from a CD-ROM or the Internet;

- undertake shared writing activities;
- view Internet resources as a class;
- discuss examples of extended writing as a class.

Interactive whiteboards ▼

The Literacy and Numeracy initiatives have highlighted the role of whole-class discussion, demonstration and shared activity between teacher and class. An interactive whiteboard uses a data projector to produce a large display that forms a type of touch screen offering the teacher a large electronic blackboard coupled to the computer. A data projector illuminates the board, which is calibrated to map the image which appears on the monitor. The teacher (or pupil) can 'write' on the board with a 'pen' or operate the Windows interface by touching the board in a similar way that the cursor would be used on the screen. The combination of whiteboard and data projector gives the teacher the opportunity to allow pupils to physically interact with the words on the board in a way that is not possible using conventional resources.

Alternative input devices ▼

There are a variety of hardware devices that provide an alternative interface to the computer. The section on special educational needs (see pages 12–13) discusses in some detail how to help pupils with specific needs.

Touch screens: these are devices that enable the user to control a computer by pointing to or touching an area of the screen. The touch screen has advantages especially when used with multimedia. With some interactive talking books, learners can point at a word and then hear it spoken.

Overlay keyboard: (also known as a concept keyboard). This is a flat board with a matrix of touch-sensitive keys. This matrix may consist of over a hundred keys, up to more than 4,000, depending upon the type of overlay keyboard. A paper overlay is placed on top of this keyboard so that when the pupil presses an area, the computer responds to the message assigned to the area. Overlay keyboards are particularly useful for pupils who cannot use a standard keyboard or find it laborious. Overlays can be prepared with whole words and phrases assigned to areas so that pupils can write text in the normal way. Whole words or chunks of pre-prepared text can be inserted by pressing a sector of the pad, saving the physical or intellectual effort of typing every word letter by letter.

Alternative mice: computer mice generally work on the principle of a rolling ball underneath the mouse making a cursor move around the screen and selections are made by pressing the buttons on the mouse. If a pupil finds using a mouse difficult, a number of variants to the mouse are available with different shapes and sizes of body and buttons, including a mouse that looks a bit like the real animal! These fit the conventional port and software programs. Trackerballs are basically upside-down mice where a mounted ball is moved by the hand. It means that less gross hand and arm movement is required.

Other alternatives include a stylus used with a graphics tablet, and a mouse pen. These will be of limited use for people with gross and fine motor movement in the arm or hand. Mouse key access utilities are available on some systems that transfer the vertical, horizontal and diagonal movements of the mouse to other keys, such as the numeric keypad.

English Software Resources ▼

For comprehensive reviews of CD-ROMs and software to support English and literacy see the review databases available through the NGfL website.

Teachers evaluating multimedia have a website containing information, evaluation and case studies based on the most popular titles: http://www.teem.org.uk

▶ KS 1 / P1-3

ABC CD-Talking Animated Alphabet
(Sherston Software)

Teaches the shapes and sounds of the alphabet through a series of animated illustrations coupled to sound. Three graded activities are customisable by the teacher:

• letter shapes;
• letter sounds;
• letter shapes and sounds.

My First Incredible Amazing Dictionary
(DK Multimedia)

A multimedia dictionary with animation, sound and graphics which develops a range of dictionary skills. An alphabet letter connects to an illustrated dictionary page on which words or pictures can be selected. Each word can be spoken and the illustrations associated with the word are animated. Links are made to words on the same subject. Great fun ideas with words! Games include:

• Guess what;
• Guess the noise;
• Insert the letter.

My World 3
(Granada Learning)

My World 3 uses a drag and drop system which develops pupils' dexterity with the mouse. There are a series of screens to support different curriculum applications which are purchased separately from the main program. Very visual and motivating for young pupils. Relevant titles include:

• Literacy – The Early Years;
• My World of Pictures and Words;
• My World in the Literacy Hour – Wordworld.

Writing With Symbols
(Widgit)

A word processor which can associate over 11,000 images to aid communication of linguistic concepts. Words can be automatically illustrated as they are typed, or pictures added as required. On-screen grids enable pupils to select words from a bank of words with or without graphics to support their writing. Other features are:

• the speech output has multiple voices;
• a pictorial spelling checker;
• pupil and teacher activities;
• records sound;
• picture addition is possible;
• supports switches for enabling physical disability.

Clicker 4
(Crick Software)

A talking word processor (*Clicker Writer*) is linked to *Clicker* which provides a series of grids from which pupils select words to support their writing. Words can be associated with clip art images. An extensive set of word lists can be supplemented from the publisher's website or added by the teacher. Pages can be saved in web-format for use on the school website.

Easy Book
(TAG)

A graphical and word processor in which pupils work on a screen formatted as an illustrated book. At the print stage the page sequencing and double siding is done automatically allowing the pupils to take away a finished book. The talking facility allows pupils to make a talking book of their own.

Encarta
(Microsoft)

A multimedia encyclopedia with excellent resources covering over 30,000 different topics. It has an interface with thousands of world wide web pages if used with a PC connected to the Internet.

Granada Writer
(Granada Learning)

A talking word processor, featuring word, picture sound and video banks. The word banks are fully editable and new banks can be added. Pages can be saved in the web-format to be viewed using a web browser (Internet Explorer) and placed on the school website. The menu bar is fully configurable and certain functions can be switched on and off to support pupils' work across the whole primary age range.

Hyperstudio
(TAG)

A comprehensive multimedia authoring program. Pages are created using a 'toolbox' which offers buttons or the identification of regular or irregular shapes to make images or parts of them into hypertext links. Links can be made to other pages, images, sounds, text, video or animation. A suite of sounds is available but other sounds can be sampled to include in the library. The simplest way to make spectacular multimedia resources which has a user interface that can be used throughout the age range.

Living Books
(Broderbund)

Living Books are the creators of interactive stories. These lively and motivating talking books highlight the words as they are spoken. Individual words are spoken by clicking on them. Each page offers an interactive multimedia experience of sound, images and animation as pupils explore the hyperlinks within the image. Excellent resources for encouraging listening and reading. School editions are available, consisting of two CD-ROMs and Teacher's Guide.

- Grandma and Me (Listening);
- Sheila Rae (Speaking);
- Arthur's Birthday (Reading);
- Little Monster at School (Writing).

Logo
(Granada Learning)

There are many versions of the *Logo* programming language available. Seymor Papert, who first developed *Logo*, called it 'thinking software'. Logo is usually associated with control of either a screen icon or a floor turtle. Pupils acquire estimation skills, and concepts such as angle and length. In an English context, the language gains come from pupils interacting with each other, using language precisely and ordering instructions.

Sherlock
(Topologika Software)

Based on the very successful *Developing Tray* program the software allows the teacher to simply construct 'cloze' procedure tasks. The pupils 'guess' the word or letter required. There are a variety of support strategies that the teacher and pupils can select. A scoring system is available that is personalised to the user. There is a suite of literacy files to teach spelling rules and aspects of grammar. Full control is given to the teacher to create customised activities to match the needs of a particular pupil. A key resource in an SEN context.

TextEase 2000
(Softease Ltd)

A talking word processor that has desktop publishing and multimedia authoring capability. The menu bar is fully configurable and certain functions can be switched on and off to support pupils' work. Pages can be saved in the web-format to be viewed using a web browser (Internet Explorer) and placed on the school website. Allows the user to click anywhere and start typing. Speech can say part words to complete documents. Other features include:

- extensive web page-creating tools;
- sound recording;
- animation creation;
- text flow around a graphic;
- text flow in frames.

Wordshark 2L
(Widgit)

A word recognition and spelling program which, through a variety of games, reinforces pupils' understanding of phonics, rhyme, homophones, prefixes, suffixes, roots and spelling rules. The 5,000 words it contains are grouped in lists to meet the developmental stages identified in the literacy hour.

▶ KS 2 / P4-7

Adobe Pagemaker
(Adobe)

A commercial desktop publishing program which offers full control over text and graphics to produce printed materials. Useful at a teacher level for a school interested in the quality of its printed materials. The electronic files will be taken directly by a commercial printer to publish documents.

Inspirations (Kidspiration)
(TAG)

Planning software that provides a simple interface to illustrate ideas and the links between them.

Microsoft FrontPage
(Microsoft)

A web authoring program offering the user full control over the creation of web pages. It produces pages that are best viewed with the latest version of Internet Explorer. A wizard is available to help the user make design decisions about layout and navigation tools. It has advanced features that support the creation of a website in addition to individual pages. The Navigation View provides a pictorial view of the site and links directly to the files from which the site is composed. An essential tool for schools developing their own websites.

Microsoft Office
(Microsoft)

Programs within the *Microsoft Office* suite are designed to be compatible. This supports OLE (object linked embedding) and cut and paste between the individual programs. This software is suitable for staff use, and older pupils.

Microsoft Publisher
(Microsoft)

A desktop publishing package with a library of useful templates to create newspapers, bi-fold leaflets, bulletins, newsletters, etc. It is mostly suited to staff use and for older pupils.

Other Microsoft titles:
Microsoft Internet Explorer
Microsoft PowerPoint (KS2 / P4-7)
Microsoft Excel (KS2 / P4-7)

Oxford Children's Encyclopedia
(Granada Learning)

A multimedia encyclopedia with topics organised in a variety of ways to allow pupils to access and organise their research. Features include:

- exploring themes;
- search by word, sound, video, picture, map, etc.;
- quizzes at 3 skill levels;
- timelines;
- a notebook to store any multimedia items selected;
- dictionary;
- bookmarking of tagged items for easy location at a later stage.

English Links in the DfEE/QCA ICT Scheme of Work ▼

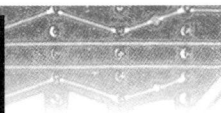

Unit	Activity	Related activities in the handbook
1B	Using a wordbank	5 Using wordbanks 10 Using word grids for writing
1C	The information around us	3 Talking books
1D	Labelling and classifying	1 Labels, captions and signs
1F	Understanding instructions and making things happen	4 Talking about control
2A	Writing stories: communicating information using text	2 Big books 10 Using word grids for writing 11 Shared writing at the computer 16 Using and generating writing frames 19 A story writer
2C	Finding information	12 Electronic dictionaries
3A	Combining text and graphics	13 Story books 14 Greetings cards
3E	E-mail	17 Writing in genre: e-mail
4A	Writing for different audiences	16 Using and generating writing frames 23 Chat, chat, chat 24 Authors at work 26 Writing in genre: sci-fi 27 Developing writers 32 Book reviews (1) 33 Book reviews (2) 34 Creating a website 37 Persuasive texts
5C	Evaluating information, checking accuracy and questioning plausibility	28 Evaluating sources: newspapers 29 Non-fiction resources
6A	Multimedia presentation	3 Talking books 25 Multimedia authoring (1) 35 Multimedia authoring (2)
6D	Using the Internet to search large databases and to interpret information	20 Researching topics 22 Ask a librarian 29 Non-fiction resources 32 Book reviews (1) 33 Book reviews (2)

The creation of separate and distinct guidelines for 5-14 Information and Communications Technology reflects many changes in society, and, therefore, in education. The increasing emphasis on the use of computer technology for word-processing, databases and spreadsheets, the power of the Internet and the acquisition of the skills required to access this powerful tool, have necessitated a change in curricula throughout Europe.

Scotland has always had a broad-based curriculum with focuses aimed at imparting the skills and knowledge for pupils to take to the next stage in their life, whatever that may be. As a reflection of this, it is important that all areas of the curriculum have links to ICT.

Nelson Thornes' ICT handbook provides the opportunity to teach many of the skills already taught using ICT in a 'real' and meaningful way. Its use of word-processing, multimedia presentation, web resources and electronic communication enhances many of the good aspects of current practice and takes the teaching of English to a new level. The activities fit well into many of the areas of the 5-14 ICT Guidelines that many teachers have struggled with.

The ICT handbooks website includes correlation charts identifying handbook activities that support the seven ICT strands.

Teachers are able to identify activities that support these strands using the ICT handbooks' website at: www.nelsonthornes.com/primary/icthandbooks.

Whilst a year group has been identified for each of the activities, many of the ICT resources and ideas can be used across the whole of a key stage or the whole primary age range; for example the use of wordbanks and writing frames.

1 Labels, Captions and Signs ▼

Learning objectives ▼

Pupils learn to:
- read, discriminate, read and spell familiar words;
- be aware of the case of letters (upper and lower).

ICT resources ▼

Word-processing programme with suitably simple interface, e.g. *Granada Writer* (Granada Learning) or *TextEase* (Softease Ltd)
Printer
Digital camera (optional)

Vocabulary ▼

caption
spell checker
clip art
shift key
caps lock
image

▼ Introduction

- Labels and captions around the classroom are often produced by the teacher to ensure clarity. In KS1/P1-3 and early KS2/P4-7 the presentation features of a word processor can provide an opportunity for pupils to label and caption classroom items and displays. The relatively small amount of letters means that the speed of typing is not too significant.
- The word processor should be set to the appropriate font, font size and colour. It is useful to know that 72 point type is an old 'inch' high. Packages such as *TextEase* and *Granada Writer* allow the pupils to place the cursor anywhere on the screen. This can be useful if they are attaching a label to clip art or a scanned image.

▼ Suggested activities

- Use a digital camera to take a picture of each pupil. Everyone takes it in turns to add their name to their own picture. These are then assembled to form a class profile. Each pupil prints out their own picture and name.
- Write captions for a class display using a large typeface (in handwriting software to produce cursive script if required).
- Produce labels for equipment around the classroom.
- Produce a sign to encourage pupils to wash their hands before eating.
- Label a local history or a science display.

▼ Assessment focus

Pupils:
- observe letter recognition at the keyboard;
- read signs and captions around the classroom.

Learning objectives ▼

Pupils learn to:
- apply their word-level skills through shared and guided reading;
- recognise features of sentences such as capital letters and punctuation;
- predict words within a sentence.

ICT resources ▼

At least a 17 inch monitor, or ideally a data projector
Presentation software such as *Microsoft PowerPoint*
TextEase 2000 (Softease Ltd), *TextEase Presenter* (Softease), *Granada Writer* (Granada Learning) or *Hyperstudio* (TAG)
Alternatively, word-processing software with the ability to import graphics
Scanner

Vocabulary ▼

clip art
image
scanner
mouse
cursor
click select
font
point size

▼ Introduction

Big books are now an established part of the shared reading activities within the literacy hour. They are expensive, and therefore the number available tends to be small. ICT can enable the teacher (and pupils) to prepare big books of their own.

This activity will only be successful if the pupils can see the text as well as they can sitting around a big book with the teacher. To achieve this, the teacher will need to use a type size that produces letters as big as those in the conventional book. A good guide it that 72 point type is an old inch high. Although the 'view' and 'zoom' features mean that a page can be enlarged, e.g. to 200%, this method can reduce the view of the whole page and its relationship with any illustrations. The use of at least a 17 inch monitor can provide a suitable picture of an A4 page that, with a suitable font, can be seen by a seated group. However, a data projector (possibly linked to an interative whiteboard) is the ideal tool for using electronic big books.

▼ Suggested activities

- Highlight words in the electronic book to illustrate features of sentences.
- Remove words and ask pupils to predict them from the sentence and story.
- Pupils generate characters for a story and the teacher interprets their ideas.
- Pupils' illustrations are used to illustrate their own story.
- Use electronic books from the Internet to give a variety of texts.

▼ Assessment focus

Pupils:
- recognise sentences and punctuation symbols and use them appropriately to give expression to their reading.

3 Talking Books ▼

Learning objectives ▼

Pupils learn to:
- reinforce and apply word level skills through shared reading;
- use a variety of strategies to predict the meaning and sense of unfamiliar words;
- identify a sentence;
- read with sufficient concentration to complete a text.

ICT resources ▼

Multimedia PC
CD-ROM
Internet access

Vocabulary ▼

image
highlight
spell checker
click select
CD-ROM
Internet
web page
mouse
animation

▼ Introduction

Talking books can be used throughout KS1/P1-3 and to support targeted SEN support at KS2/P4-7. Talking books are multimedia resources, usually on CD-ROM but increasingly available on the Internet. Words are brought to life by being read and through the animations available on each page. Words and phrases are usually highlighted as they are read, helping pupils to understand how to progress through texts from left to right.

Although talking books are usually associated with Year R/P1, they can provide support and encouragement for older, slow readers who can use the resources independently in English sessions to sharpen their reading and word recognition skills. Exploring the interactive version of a familiar story can promote discussion and thus the use of oral language.

▼ Suggested activities

- Pupils read the text with the sound turned off and then hear it being read and assess their own reading.
- Invite pupils to name the characters and predict 'what will happen next' before clicking around the screen.
- Make a tape recording of the story from the 'real book' version as though it would be the CD-ROM reading.
- Visit the website of some characters from talking books, e.g. Arthur and friends.

▼ Assessment focus

Pupils:
- read with more meaning and expression;
- observe word recognition;
- are able to predict endings of sentences.

4 Talking about Control ▼

Learning objectives ▼

Pupils learn to:
- use language precisely;
- sequence words for meaning;
- frame a set of instructions;
- use the appropriate register in writing instructions.

ICT resources ▼

Control vehicle (Pip, Pixie or Roamer) (KS1)
Control software such as *Logo* (Granada Learning) (KS2) and computer peripherals such as lights and buzzers

Vocabulary ▼

sequence
instructions
options
order
robot
control
command
sensor

▼ Introduction

Controlling on-screen icons or control devices such as a floor turtle provides a vehicle for even young pupils to use directional language such as 'forwards' and 'backwards', 'right' and 'left' turns. It also develops spatial awareness and the ability to estimate distance and angle of turn. The learning can be described as play, investigative learning or problem solving. The demands of learning in this way require a high level of language.

To support special educational needs, control activity can be empowering for those pupils with limited motor skills or limited concentration. At an individual level, success can be highly motivating. Working within a group allows the strengths of each pupil to be recognised.

▼ Suggested activities

Introduce tasks initially as a small group activity.
- Give a suggested scenario which will lead to storytelling based around a character. The robot can become the postman's van visiting different numbered or coloured houses. The 'robot' can be 'dressed up' by adding a card shape to the basic box, and lights and buzzers can be added.
- Guide the robot around a plan of the school drawn out on the floor.
- Frame a sequence of commands for other pupils to follow, which will steer them around an obstacle course in the school hall or playground.
- Create a control sequence to make a geometric shape using *Logo*.
- For more able pupils, they can investigate left and right, use simple grids to follow and design their own maps.
- To meet a variety of abilities, let each person have a turn at suggesting developments to the control routine.

▼ Assessment focus

Pupils:
- use precise language in framing commands;
- are able to sequence words.

5 Using Wordbanks ▼

Learning objectives ▼

Pupils learn to:
- read on sight high frequency words identified for the age group;
- use wordbanks as a resource for writing and improving spelling;
- collect new words from reading and work in other subjects.

ICT resources ▼

Word processor
Floppy disk
Shared network drive

Vocabulary ▼

speech function
wordbank
select
insert
copy and paste
table
template

▼ Introduction

Wordbanks are simply a collection of words available to the user to select from as they write. Pupils will be familiar with the concept through their 'word book'.

There are a variety of ways in which the teacher can make a wordbank available to pupils to aid their writing.

Granada Writer (and *TextEase*) provide the capacity to create wordbanks. The words can be used in the working area of the processor by selecting them. These banks are best done by the teacher. The talking facility is an additional aid to word recognition.

Off-line banks can also be pre-prepared by the teacher using the 'tables' function in *Microsoft Word*. These are saved on a floppy disk, stored on the local PC or made available through a public network drive. They are coded with the topic and year group. Pupils write their story selecting from the printed words and adding their own. They can use the word directly from the bank if they use the copy and paste commands.

Pupils can use the provisional nature of the word-processing files to collect and revise sets of words based on particular subjects.

▼ Suggested activities

- Pupils download a bank of words associated with a topic, e.g. story characters/plot or non-fiction, e.g. the Romans. The bank is available for all computer-based writing.
- Pupils prepare their own wordbanks based on, for example, the week's spellings, the frequency words identified for the year, reading books or topics in other subjects.

▼ Assessment focus

- Use of words on constructed sentences in printed work.
- Wordbanks created by pupils.

Learning objectives ▼

Pupils learn to:
- discriminate all three phonemes in CVC word;
- form letters correctly;
- identify and spell words with consonant clusters;
- blend phonemes in words with cluster when reading.

ICT resources ▼

Access to the Internet on one or more computers
Printer

Vocabulary ▼

website
Internet
mouse
select
cursor
keyboard

▼ Introduction

- Aligned to the BBC TV series *Words and Pictures Plus*, this web resource provides a range of interactive games and activities to support pupils in learning phonics. The content includes:
  - CVC words;
  - consonant clusters;
  - long vowel sounds;
  - high frequency words.
- The high frequency words support vocabulary and spelling throughout KS1/P1-3. The *Magic Pencil* feature allows pupils to practise correct letter orientation, formation and proportion in their handwriting. There is also a resource and guidance section for parents and teachers.

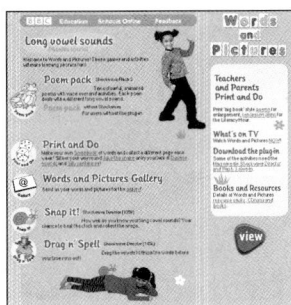

Web address: www.bbc.co.uk/education

▼ Suggested activities

- Pupils use the 'Gallery' feature to submit their work.
- Use the printable resources to develop phonic skills.
- Use the *Magic Pencil* feature to support handwriting skills.

▼ Assessment focus

- Use a teaching assistant to check pupils' progress with activities on the site.
- Assess the printed materials produced by pupils.

7 Sorting Words ▼

Learning objectives ▼

Pupils learn to:
- recognise the importance of correct sequence;
- organise words alphabetically using the first two letters;
- write simple instructions.

ICT resources ▼

Word processor
Printer

Vocabulary ▼

table
highlight
select
sort
word list
drag and drop
copy and paste

▼ Introduction

Card sort ordering of words with handwritten or typed cards can be replicated on the computer using a variety of word processors. Using a generic application such as *Microsoft Word*, it is best to constrain the words to a table. The 'tables' function in Word is a powerful feature and well worth learning for making planning tools, etc.

In this context, the cells of a two-column table are used to accept words which can be moved from a selection provided by the teacher. The pupils double click on the word to select it and then use the cut and paste icons to place it in the numbered box. With greater dexterity, pupils can use the 'drag and drop' feature to shuffle words from one box to the next.

Tables can also be used to sort words alphabetically, using the table > sort command in *MS Word*. In *TextEase 2000* and *Granada Writer* the words are treated as graphics and so can be moved around similar to magnetic words. This provides an accessible, but less formal sort for younger pupils.

▼ Suggested activities

- Rearrange a set of instructions on the screen into the correct order, e.g. instructions for making a sandwich.
- Pupils sort a jumbled table of words alphabetically with the two initial letters into the next column using the copy and paste. Finally, use the table > sort command to sort the initial list. Check if ordering was correct. Suggestions:
  - order days of the week or months of the year;
  - reorder sentences;
  - group beginnings and endings from a number of stories using the 'cut and paste' feature;
  - jumble up the lines of a well-known rhyme and ask pupils to reorder it.

▼ Assessment focus

- Print out completed sorting activities for assessment.

Learning objectives ▼

Pupils learn:
- verb endings such as 'ing' or 'ed';
- sentence components such as nouns;
- to segment words into phonemes to aid spelling;
- how to apply common suffixes such as 'ful' or 'ly'.

ICT resources ▼

Presentation software with animation function, such as
TextEase Presenter (Softease)
Microsoft PowerPoint
Data projector or large monitor

Vocabulary ▼

animation
slide
effects

▼ Introduction

Presentation software can support word and sentence level work by allowing pupils to see the components of words or sentences being constructed. To create the animation, teachers use the 'text box' feature from the drawing toolbar to create the word or sentence component. The box can then be dragged into position to complete the word or sentence.

The 'Slide Show – Custom' animation feature allows multiple elements to be selected for animation. The 'Effects' offers a variety of ways in which the components will be added to the word or sentence, e.g. 'Dissolve in' or 'Fly in'.

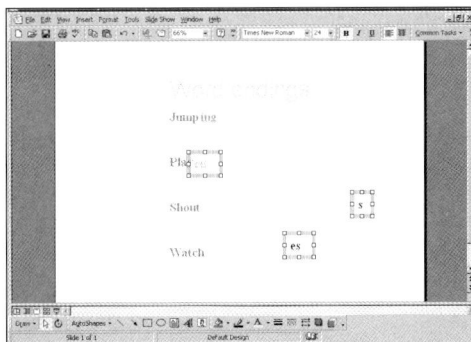

▼ Suggested activities

Screen dump from PowerPoint
- Animate verb endings such as 'ing' or 'ed'.
- Animate sentence components such as nouns.
- Segment words into phonemes for spelling.
- Illustrate examples of words and phrases that link sentences, e.g. after, meanwhile, during.
- Show matching verbs to nouns/pronouns.
- Apply common suffixes such as 'ful' or 'ly'.

▼ Assessment focus

- Teacher takes pupils' suggestions before running animation.

9 Writing with Symbols ▼

Learning objectives ▼

Pupils learn to:
- locate words by their initial letter;
- use knowledge of grammar to predict words based on the context;
- recognise words and their meaning.

ICT resources ▼

Software such as: *Writing with Symbols* and *Inclusive Writer* (both Widgit Software)
Clicker (Crick Software)
Printer (optional)

Vocabulary ▼

symbols/pictures
wordlist
clip art
illustration

▼ Introduction

Very young pupils and those who have difficulties with word recognition, spelling or comprehension can be supported with picture symbols and sounds. Symbols are an everyday part of children's culture, however understanding the symbols can depend on culture and context. Seeing a word accompanied by a symbol can reassure the reader and increase confidence.

Specialised software such as *Writing with Symbols* and *Inclusive Writer* provide libraries of symbols that go beyond simple clip art associated with everyday objects. *Writing with Symbols* has full Rebus and PCS symbol libraries which, in the context of enabling pupils with auditory impairment, can extend pupils' experience with sign language. A similar resource can be provided through the use of 'Clicker grids'.

▼ Suggested activities

- An adult helper/teaching assistant works with a pupil acting as the 'scribe', transferring their choices to the computer.
- Use the symbol generator to add labels to familiar objects in the classroom.
- From the choices offered by the teacher, pupils select those groups of words which begin with the same initial letter.
- The teacher/helper selects a series of symbols and helps the pupil to read the 'script'. The pupil then selects words from the 'bank' to match the symbols. The teacher/helper then enters them if necessary.
- Pictures of pupils, teacher or personal objects/animals can be generated to work within the symbol library. Recorded sounds and speech can be added to reinforce the meaning of the symbol.

▼ Assessment focus

- Printed output from the software.
- Observation of the pupil's ability to synchronise symbols and words.

10 Using Word Grids for Writing ▼

Learning objectives ▼

Pupils learn to:
- construct simple sentences based around familiar words selected from a bank of words;
- recognise familiar words;
- read on sight and use words from the year list;
- sort/classify words to particular criteria, e.g. rhyming, antonyms or similar roots.

ICT resources ▼

Word bank software, such as *Clicker* (Crick Software)
Wordbanks provided by software or created by the teacher
Printer

Vocabulary ▼

word bank
word grid
speech function
select
edit
insert
spacebar
shift
delete

▼ Introduction

Programmes such as *Clicker* or *WordBar* offer the teacher a way of providing a bank of words and images that pupils can use at word or sentence level. These are often referred to as word grids. The grid resources take the tedium out of writing and make the best use of the 15 minutes available in the literacy hour for independent work. Clicking on the word or picture inserts it into the writing page. Editing is done in the usual way. The software works well with overlay keyboards and switches in a SEN context.

Writing using a word grid can offer a stimulating resource for pupils who struggle to write at length. The print-outs allow the pupil to have something worthwhile to show at the end of 15 minutes.

For younger pupils, grids associated with familiar books and characters from their reading scheme will be more appealing. The software supplies some example banks, but teachers can progress to developing their own grids to meet specific identified needs. Further banks are often available on the suppliers' Internet site, e.g. *CrickSoft*. New words introduced in the context of another subject, e.g. science, can be made available for writing and recording.

▼ Suggested activities

- Use a grid provided with the software to support pupils' sentence construction around their reading scheme in the 15 minutes individual time.
- Make a grid with a collection of words that have to be sorted into groups of one, two and three syllable words.
- Provide third person pronouns and a sentence where the noun is replaced by a word in the grid.
- Finding words that rhyme. Pupils find words that they think rhyme and write a sentence, e.g. 'Bat rhymes with mat'.

▼ Assessment focus

- Print out composed text for assessment

📖 YEAR 2 / P3

Learning objectives ▼

Pupils learn to:
- write stories using simple settings;
- write alternative sequels to known stories;
- take account of grammar and punctuation.

ICT resources ▼

Word-processing software
Printer
Data projector or large monitor
Wordbank or grid (optional)

Vocabulary ▼

word processor(s)
spell checker
wordbank
save
file
clip art

▼ Introduction

As part of shared reading and writing, the class can create a story together, using a word processor with a data projector or large monitor. The provisional capability of word-processing software enables the teacher to take the pupils' ideas and add them into the story. Pupils can be asked to make suggestions and refinements.

The activity can also be undertaken by groups of pupils who, over a period of time, can add to, and if necessary revise their contributions if only one computer is available. If the 'stages in stories' have been taught, pupils can be assigned to write for beginnings, middles or ends.

▼ Suggested activities

- Type in a short introduction to the story (story starters can be found on the Internet, e.g. *Magic Pen Starters Page*). Start by explaining the activity and reading through the introduction. Pupils suggest an idea or a sentence to add. At the end of the process the teacher can read the completed story.
- As an extension to the literacy hour, the activity can be run over the week with pupils (in groups) taking turns to add to a story. Adult support at the reading stage may be required. The spell checker should be set to check words as they are entered. A suitable bank of words can be provided by the teacher if the software supports word banks (grids).
- Use clip art or scan in illustrations drawn by the pupils to enhance the presentation. If the printer is available, give each pupil a copy of the story.

▼ Assessment focus

- Assess pupils' contribution to class discussion.
- Pupils mark their contribution on a printed copy of the story.
- Monitor individual work through observing discussion at the computer.

Learning objectives ▼

Pupils learn how to:
- search a dictionary using alphabetical or other search criteria;
- find the meaning of words;
- explore definitions and the origins of words.

ICT resources ▼

CD-ROM dictionary
Web-based dictionary
Multimedia PC

Vocabulary ▼

CD-ROM
website
navigation
search
index
enter
clip art
illustration
find-replace

▼ Introduction

CD-ROM dictionaries enable pupils to find words, meaning, related words, and grammatically similar words, e.g. words beginning with particular sounds, easily. This is a motivating way to begin to use alphabetical lists of words and can be available in the classroom alongside printed dictionaries. Multimedia CD-ROMs can also 'say' the words the pupils find, enabling them to check that their choice is correct.

On the Internet, a picture dictionary such as *Little Explorers* – a picture dictionary with links or for older pupils www.yourdictionary.com – has sections on homophones, anagrams, antonyms, synonyms, word oddities and a wonderful section on grammar and fun and games with words.

▼ Suggested activities

- Create a writing frame to direct pupils to specific aspects of the dictionary.
- As part of whole-class or group work sessions in the literacy hour, find the meaning of specific words or related words.
- Explore homonyms using the 'multiple meanings' feature.
- Use the thesaurus or dictionary to explore alternative words for use in a story.

▼ Assessment focus

- Observe ability to use alphabetical order to find words in dictionary work.
- Assess the use of wordsearches in written work.
- Pupils understand the term 'synonym';
- Pupils select synonyms that are appropriate for the context and style of text.

13 Story Books ▼

Learning objectives ▼

Pupils learn to:
- make simple picture storybooks with sentences, modelling them on basic text conventions, e.g. cover, author's name, title, layout, etc.
- re-read their own work for sense and punctuation.

ICT resources ▼

Word-processing software, such as *Granada Writer* (Granada Learning), *TextEase* (Softease Ltd),
Internet access (optional)
Colour printer

Vocabulary ▼

image
highlight
spell checker
click select
CD-ROM
Internet
web page
mouse
animation
text

▼ Introduction

For young pupils, the combination of few words and a clear illustration is important in deciphering the meaning of text. Word processors designed for children offer them the opportunity to produce simple books with the features of conventional books. The print-out has clarity and can support pupils whose handwriting is still undeveloped.

The 'pages' are best created as a template (e.g. using frames in *TextEase* to constrain where the pupils write). The graphics for an illustrated story book can come from clip art or be 'borrowed' from a website. Alternatively the pupils' own drawings can be scanned and imported onto the page. Using a word processor, teacher or pupils can fill out the story. Websites, such as Sebastian Swan on the Kent NGfL site illustrate the potential of web-based story books.

▼ Suggested activities

- Provide a template using a word processor or presentation software with suitable pictures scanned or imported from the web.
- Pupils retell a familiar story and generate a big book with their own words. They enter the text of their story alongside the picture.
- Working as a class, the stages for a familiar story are allocated to groups who each make one page of the book. Illustrations are drawn by the pupils and scanned in.

▼ Assessment focus

- Printed page(s) from story book.
- Pages of an electronic story book.

14 Greetings Cards ▼

Learning objectives ▼

Pupils learn to:
- recognise that certain types of text are targeted at particular readers;
- identify different patterns of rhyme in poetry.

ICT resources ▼

Word processor
Colour printer
Optional:
Scanner
Digital camera
DTP package
Internet
Word grids

Vocabulary ▼

Internet
e-mail
attachment
website
search engine
download
image
graphic
DTP
author
clip art
text
colour printer

▼ Introduction

Images, graphics and text can be combined to form cards for celebrations and festivals throughout the year. For younger pupils, a few fixed templates prepared with images from which the pupils can select, can provide the vehicle for pupils to enter a limited amount of text. *MS Publisher* has ready prepared templates. *PowerPoint* handles images/clip art and text well and provides a number of designs for slides which can be usefully adapted for use in preparing a card.

Word banks with associated clip art, created by the teacher, can help support the range of ability with sentence and spelling.

Electronic postcards have become a popular way of sending greetings. Sites such as www.bluemountain.com provide free facilities for making and sending electronic greetings cards. There are plenty of cards produced by children to choose from, and the chance to submit new ones.

▼ Suggested activities

- Investigate a range of greetings cards suitable for children. Take the style of the poem or rhyme and write a new card using the illustration(s) provided (by the teacher).
- Use a digital camera to take pictures of pupils, who are each given a photograph and asked to produce an individualised card for that person, incorporating the photo.
- Groups work on ideas for a class card and vote for the one they like best to be produced. All pupils receive one copy to send home.
- Pupils use a poem they have written and add it to an electronic template on the web to send an e-card.
- Identify a number of different audiences for greetings cards and develop a card to suit a particular group.

▼ Assessment focus

- Copies of written poem, verse or greeting.
- Print-out of card.
- Print-out of e-card sent to other pupils.

Learning objectives ▼

Pupils learn:
- predictive reading skills;
- word recognition;
- how words affects meaning;
- grammatical awareness.

ICT resources ▼

Sherlock (Topologika) or similar text disclosure software
Multimedia computer

Vocabulary ▼

speech function
text
replace

▼ Introduction

Sherlock is an example of software that allows teachers to remove letters or words from a text. This software builds on the very successful *Developing Tray*. Whilst this can be done in a word processor, this software offers additional features.

Finding the right letter or word can be done as a type of 'hangman' exercise. Pupils can 'peep' if they get stuck, or it can speak a letter or word. An optional scoring system provides a motivating system encouraging pupils to work against the clock or choose more difficult tasks (and thus gain more points) as they make progress.

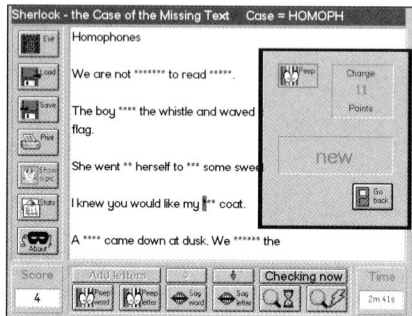

The teacher's pages offer a range of texts, but also allow any text to be entered and then customised against a series of options. Worksheets can be produced if printed exercises are required to supplement computer-based work.

▼ Suggested activities

- Hide all vowels or consonants at a selected interval.
- Remove all full stops and/or capital letters.
- Remove speech marks from text with dialogue.
- Add pictures to give clues to missing words in the text.

▼ Assessment focus

- Observe progress with the task at the computer.
- Record scores provided by the program.

Learning objectives ▼

Pupils learn to:
- make simple notes from non-fiction text;
- plan the stages when writing a story;
- map out text showing development and structure;
- use writing frames to develop points of view with illustrations and examples.

ICT resources ▼

Word processor
Clip art
Electronic non-fiction resources, e.g. CD-ROM or Internet (optional)

Vocabulary ▼

clip art
CD-ROM
writing frame
form
table
cells

▼ Introduction

Recording or writing frames (writing grids) are a common feature of literacy work, but are useful across most curriculum areas to give a structure to pupils' organisation of information they collect. Frames can support differentiation when they contain different amounts of guidance on non-fiction research questions and help the organisation of information. The addition of attractive graphics and clip art can offer visual clues and produce a more interesting backdrop to the pupils' written ideas.

When pupils' keyboard skills are developed sufficiently to enable them to type in text at a satisfying rate, writing frames can be provided to be completed on the computer. This allows the importing of text from sources such as CD-ROMs and the Internet. It is possible to lock the size of a 'text entry box' to constrain the amount pupils write, thus encouraging them to be selective about the amount of information they present from their research.

▼ Suggested activities

- Planning the stages in a story: provide the initial idea and ending, and pupils fill in the stages inbetween.
- Summarise a chapter of a book or a complete story.
- Write a book review.
- Writing in different genre can be supported through the use of frames:
  - forming an opinion on an issue, e.g. environmental;
  - writing a set of instructions or a procedure, e.g. making a kite in Design and Technology;
  - scaffolding the extraction of information from a CD-ROM or Internet encylopedia, e.g. Roman food;
  - developing persuasive text, e.g. supporting homeless people;
  - recounting a visit, e.g. to a local museum.

▼ Assessment focus

- Completed frames that are handwritten or completed on the computer.

▼ Introduction

E-mail text messaging has quickly established its own idiom. As pupils are learning the conventions of correct use of the language, the lack of punctuation conventions, abbreviations and symbols, e.g. emoticons, challenges their use of standard English.

A digital camera enables the communication to extend into descriptive pieces associated with pictures, e.g. of the locality. A scanner enables pupils to send their drawings and paintings to the recipients.

There are an increasing number of sites which offer an 'ask the expert' service. These include libraries, companies, scientific research establishments, artists and musicians. The class teacher can establish pen pals in another school through a web service, e.g. www.kidlink.org

Warning: pupils must not allow themselves to be identified through photographs. E-mail recipients should be vetted by the teacher, and pupils warned of responding to strangers attempting to communicate with them. Class or group responses and photographs are safer.

▼ Suggested activities

At KS1/P1-3 pupils should prepare their messages and replies on paper or at a word processor and only go on-line when their ideas are in electronic format can be quickly processed. At KS2/P4-7, messages can be via the e-mail client itself.
- Through reading print-outs of a variety of e-mails the class investigates some of the features of the genre.
- Pupils compose class letters on e-mail and compare the replies.
- Establish links with a school in a contrasting type of location, e.g. inner city and rural, or in a different country.
- Send an e-mail expressing a view on a current issue to a radio programme such as Radio 4's *Today* programme.

▼ Assessment focus

- Printed e-mails and replies sent/received.

Learning objectives ▼

Pupils learn to:
- read and follow simple instructions;
- discuss the merits and limitations of instructional texts;
- read letters written for particular purposes and investigate the form, layout and style.

ICT resources ▼

Access to the Internet on one or more computers
Printer

Vocabulary ▼

website
Internet
list
instructions
collection
template

▼ Introduction

The British Library have created a website which encourages the creation of books and other printed material. Its resources show words used in a variety of genres from advertisements to comics and different types of instructions encountered in everyday life. The resources of the library show how these have changed over time. Activities on the site include:
- Writing instructions.
- Following instructions.
- The teachers' zone contains a growing set of resources such as making books of various types, e.g. scrolls.
- Displaying the written word.

Schools need to register to use the school project zone where work can be submitted. Web address: www.blewa.co.uk

▼ Suggested activities

- Make a 'different' type of book following the instructions provided, e.g. scroll, folded.
- Look at the Victorian advertisements and then write a persuasive advertisement in a Victorian style.
- Create a short comic strip with captions based on a comic in the collection.
- Compose a set of instructions in the style of those provided to make another object.
- Members of a group assume the different roles required to create a small folded book for a chain of fast food restaurants.
- Select a letter from the collection and write a letter in a similar style.

▼ Assessment focus

- Quality of books produced when following instructions provided.
- Print-out of instructions written by pupils.
- Interactions between members of the group involved in creating a book.

19 A Story Writer ▼

Learning objectives ▼

Pupils learn to:
- use alternative words and expressions that are more accurate or interesting than common choices;
- investigate the extent to which words can be altered without changing the meaning of a text;
- reinforce word and sentence level skills in shared writing.

ICT resources ▼

Word processor compatible with a Spreadsheet e.g. *Microsoft Word* and *Microsoft Excel*
Printer
Internet access (optional)

Vocabulary ▼

website
cell
text entry box
linking

▼ Introduction

- Websites, such as Squigly's Writing Corner (www.squiglysplayhouse.com/WritingCorner) offer pupils the opportunity to add elements of a story. These are inserted in some existing short stories automatically. Pupils can edit the elements until it makes the story they require.
- Pupils can then evaluate the result and modify words until it makes sense. The story can be printed or copied into a word processor.
- A word processor such as *Microsoft Word* that supports Object Linking & Embedding (OLE) can be used to make a story writer that is available in the classroom. The stories are controlled by the teacher with decisions made by the pupils. OLE allows data (such as words) in one application (spreadsheet) to be linked into a document in another application (word processor). Pupils enter the words in cells against the type of word required, e.g. a name, a noun or a verb. To only allow the pupils to enter names in the cells provided, the rest of the sheet should be locked. Find out how to do this using the Help system in Excel.

▼ Suggested activities

- Classroom assistant works with a small group asking the questions, offering examples of adjectives, verbs, nouns, etc. and enters the words. The pupils listen to the story being read to them and suggest modifications.
- Teacher uses suggestions from the class during shared reading and writing session to use a Web or PC-based Story Maker.

▼ Assessment focus

- Printed stories.
- Observation of pupils' suggestions.

20 Researching Topics ▼

Learning objectives ▼

Pupils learn to:
- turn statements into questions;
- pose and record questions prior to reading non-fiction texts;
- scan text for key words or phrases;
- evaluate the usefulness of text.

ICT resources ▼

CD-ROM encyclopedia or non-fiction subject-focused resource
Internet running a suitable free-text search engine such as *Ask Jeeves for Kids*

Vocabulary ▼

database
record
index
search engine
CD-ROM
key words
data entry form

▼ Introduction

Before pupils can find answers from electronic (or printed) sources of information they need to learn to devise questions. In the early years the teacher usually frames the question, e.g. 'Where do tigers live?'. As their research skills develop, pupils will need to reformulate information requirements. When pupils are using non-fiction information resources on CD-ROM or searching the Internet with a search engine, there is ample opportunity to meet literacy objectives. Research activity may be done outside the literacy hour in the context of other subjects, e.g. science.

Most CD-ROM resources, e.g. *The Vikings* (Anglia Multimedia Ltd) use a key wordsearch tool and other browsing options such as timelines or index to lead the user to relevant information. On the Internet, free-text search engines such as *Ask Jeeves for Kids* encourages the user to pose a question as a sentence rather than isolated words, e.g. *What happened to the monasteries during the reign of Henry VIII?* becomes *Henry +Tudor* in other search engines such as Yahoo.

▼ Suggested activities

Strategies for developing questions to support a range of ability include:
- Brainstorming: write down a number of questions, eliminate until only two remain.
- Mind mapping: draw a diagram to represent what is known and then formulate questions to find new information.
- Use prompts in writing frames as a means of encouraging question generation, organisation and evaluation of the data collected.

▼ Assessment focus

- Written record of questions asked.
- Check CD-ROM 'search history' provides record of route taken.
- Print out the search engine page which produced the 'best sources' found.

21 Mapping Ideas ▼

Learning objectives ▼

Pupils learn:
- how arguments are presented – ordering points and linking them together;
- to plot a sequence of episodes as a plan for writing;
- to fill out brief notes into connected prose;
- to collect information and present it in a simple format (diagrammatic).

ICT resources ▼

Word processor
Graphics software, such as *Granada Draw* (Granada Learning)
Planning software, such as *Kidspiration* (TAG) (optional)
Printer

Vocabulary ▼

links
view
diagram
outline
graphics
dragging
instructions
sequence
symbol

▼ Introduction

Diagrams and concept maps (mind maps) can help pupils develop and organise their ideas when writing. *Inspiration* (and now *Kidspiration*) is a software application that was developed to support 'thinking'. It makes it relatively simple to produce diagrams with links and comments. Unlike pen and paper/board/flipchart techniques, the software makes editing and reorganising simple. The diagram view can be transformed into a writing view where text is organised in a hierarchy called an 'outline' (headings are arranged in terms of their weight). Pupils can write their piece under the headings. Dragging a box in the diagram to a different level will move the heading and text associated with it in the outline.

Thinking software can help pupils who find organising and retaining ideas difficult. Dyspraxia and dyslexia challenge pupils' organisational ability. See www.inspirations.com for more detail.

▼ Suggested activities

- The class brainstorms ideas at the start of a topic and records their ideas as a series of unconnected 'bubbles'.
- Given a set of randomly associated ideas for a story, pupils work in small groups to organise and make links between them. Each pupil has a print-out of the group's ideas.
- Given a print-out of the class's ideas as a chart, pupils write a story or report.
- Given a random set of instructions, the class suggests how to sequence them.
- In groups, pupils construct a mind map of a book the class is currently working on. Groups compare their maps and critically evaluate each one.

▼ Assessment focus

Pupils are able to:
- understand how paragraphs or chapters are used to collect, order and build ideas;
- read flowcharts to explain a process;
- understand and explain the way ideas are linked together.

22 Ask a Librarian ▼

Learning objectives ▼

Pupils learn:
- how to frame a question for another person to answer;
- how to acknowledge sources of information used in their own work;
- to use library catalogues to locate books.

ICT resources ▼

Web access
Printer

Vocabulary ▼

information source
website
web page
electronic form
library catalogue (OPAC)

▼ Introduction

The People's Network initiative is developing public libraries into places where children can access electronic resources alongside books, cassettes and videos.
Initiatives in libraries include:
– homework clubs: a quiet place to study;
– readers' clubs: librarians are experts in Reader Development (encouraging readers to a wider range of authors);
   Many libraries now have a web-based library catalogue which can be searched through the Internet.

▼ Suggested activities

- Pupils can ask research questions through the 'Ask a librarian' website (www.ask-a-librarian.org.uk). Answers include a reference to where the information was located.
- Groups of pupils frame questions and pose them for the 'librarian'.
- Address the question: How should you acknowledge the source of your ideas when they come from someone/ somewhere else?
- Pupils visit the local library and pose a similar question. Compare the answers from each of the sources. Use the Library Catalogue (OPAC) to search for predetermined books.
- Search web-based library catalogues (OPACs) to locate books.

▼ Assessment focus

Pupils:
- print out the reply that contains the question for the teacher to assess;
- use a library catalogue to locate books;
- understand why sources should be acknowledged.

23 Chat, Chat, Chat ▼

Learning objectives ▼

Pupils:
- learn to write notes and messages linked to other work in the school;
- understand the difference between formal and informal texts;
- learn to select a style of writing appropriate to the intended reader.

ICT resources ▼

Internet access
Registration with chat or messenger facility and installation of any required software

Vocabulary ▼

text entry
keypad
Internet chat
messaging service

▼ Introduction

Very few pupils arrive at school unfamiliar with the immediacy of messaging services via mobile phones. The 'language' of mobile phones has a synergy with early writing, employing phonic roots to create a shorthand suitable for the rather laborious entry via a mobile phone keypad.

Chat services make up a substantial proportion of Internet traffic. Whilst it would be ill-advised to allow young pupils to have open access to chat services, where the teacher can control the traffic between sender and recipient the results can be productive. Chat rooms allow access to the visitor who can join in the general discussion without being identified. To organise synchronous (simultaneous) chat between members of a class, a network of computers is required.

The search engine Yahooligans.com also offers well-controlled chat and messenger environments and excellent guidance for teachers and parents.

▼ Suggested activities

- Ask the group a question and then each station sends the answer as quickly as possible to the teacher's PC.
- A station sets a question which is then sent to a particular recipient. This can be passed on or answered by the recipient. All groups can send a question. At the end of the session a tally is made of the recipients who provided the most correct answers.
- A station describes a person and then recipients are asked to write a reply in a style appropriate to the situation and status of the person.
- On the Internet, chat with a scientist, entertainer or artist. (Check that the website has a good pedigree before encouraging pupils to use it, and send from a class not individuals.)

▼ Assessment focus

- Print-out of relevant messages, chat strands and observation of contributions.

24 Authors at Work ▼

Learning objectives ▼

Pupils learn:
- how to write in the style of an author;
- to be familiar with some established authors and identify what is special about their work;
- to review a range of stories and authors.

ICT resources ▼

Internet access
Website
E-mail

Vocabulary ▼

author
Internet
website
planning software

▼ Introduction

The fashion for most popular films and music to have a website is increasingly being followed by successful authors. Publishers are aware of the power of establishing a cult status which can be achieved if the author is accessible and 'real'. Websites for major publishers and on-line bookshops are a good place to start looking for authors on-line. Try www.storiesfromtheweb.org

▼ Suggested activities

From the site:
- Explore the range of work of the author.
- Investigate any reviews that are connected to the author's work.
- Read web-based interviews with authors.
- E-mail or enter a chat room with an author: find out how the author obtains ideas for his or her characters. Find out how he or she develops a plot or a sequence of events in a story.
- What kind of planning tools does he or she engage in? Brainstorming? Mind mapping?
- How does he or she use ICT in his or her work?
- Attach a short passage written in the style of the author and ask for comment.

▼ Assessment focus

Pupils can:
- use a variety of strategies for developing ideas and characters for a story;
- identify some established authors and talk about their work and why they are appealing;
- discuss style and attempt to emulate it in their own writing.

25 Multimedia Authoring (1) ▼

Learning objectives ▼

Pupils learn to:
- describe and sequence key incidents in a variety of ways;
- collaborate with others to write stories for a particular audience;
- present a point of view linking points persuasively, selecting style and vocabulary;
- write non-chronological reports linked to other subjects.

ICT resources ▼

Presentation software such as *PowerPoint* (Microsoft)
Multimedia PC
Web browser (optional)
Internet access (optional)

Vocabulary ▼

presentation
multimedia
image
menu
icons
hyperlink
action buttons
sound samples
graphic
animation
sound
slide
sequence
effects

▼ Introduction

Presentation software such as *PowerPoint* can support pupils creating text for specific uses or audiences, e.g. creating an interactive sequence to accompany a school exhibition.

Although as a piece of presentation software *PowerPoint* is usually used to display a linear sequence of slides, it also has an 'Action Buttons' feature which enable slides to be linked in any order. Multimedia resources, such as sound effects, clip art and animation effects are available in the programme or can be created. Coupled with a range of templates and themes pupils can create a motivating set of resources.

▼ Suggested activities

- Pupils experiment with the features of the programme and develop a set of linked slides:
  - Animation, graphics and multimedia effects such as sound can be added to the slides.
  - A linear sequence can be established using the 'Slide Sorter'.
  - Action Buttons allow any slide to be linked to any other.
  - The Slide Show-Custom animation feature allows multiple elements to be selected for animation.
  - The Effects menu offers a variety of ways that the components will be added to the word or sentence e.g. 'Dissolve in' or 'Fly in'.
- Create an interactive story where choices determine the outcomes.
- Develop a resource to support an exhibition, e.g. a collection of local historical artefacts.
- Save *PowerPoint* slides in a web format and viewed in a browser as a set of web pages (on the school intranet).

▼ Assessment focus

- Slide show as an electronic file demonstrated to the class or published on the school website.

26 Writing in Genre: Sci-fi ▼

Learning objectives ▼

Pupils:
- understand techniques of how to create imaginary worlds;
- learn the features of a genre (sci-fi);
- discuss the appeal of a particular book or character;
- write in the style of an author.

ICT resources ▼

Internet access
Word processor such as *Granada Writer* (Granada Learning)
Clicker grid (optional)

Vocabulary ▼

Internet
key words
e-mail
attachment
website
search engine
discussion group
download
image
author
compose
text

▼ Introduction

Science fiction and fantasy material abounds on the web. Pupils can search using key words for 'amateur' or professional writers. Publishers' websites are a rich source of information, as are on-line bookshops. Images can be obtained to support fantasy writing using search engines that offer 'searching by media'.

   Much of the adult material that will be compiled in an Internet search may contain unsuitable material and it is therefore advised that only vetted sites are used.

▼ Suggested activities

- Locate three sources of science fiction stories on the web. Individual pupils or groups select the story that most appeals to them and explain their choice to the class.
- Pupils create their own 'alien character' and decide attributes. Their own drawings, or a downloaded image(s) of a sci-fi character from the web can be used as illustrations to enhance their new story.
- Use a clicker grid for new or difficult to spell science/technology words to aid drafting for pupils with a limited vocabulary. Import text into DTP program.
- Talk to a sci-fi author or read an interview on bookshop or publishers' websites to see what they say about their work, e.g. Terry Pratchett.
- Take part in an e-mail or web-conference discussion on a particular author with other pupils from the same or another school.

▼ Assessment focus

- Character description written in a writing frame.
- Printed description of sci-fi character.
- Printed stories created.
- Record of replies from sci-fi author's website.

Learning objectives ▼

Pupils:
- learn to write new scenes or characters into a story maintaining consistency of characters and style;
- understand the aspects of narrative structure;
- use a range of strategies for planning stories.

ICT resources ▼

Internet access
Word processor
Printer

Vocabulary ▼

website
submission form
word-count

▼ Introduction

The Literacy Trust maintains a selective range of links to sites which can develop pupils' writing skills: www.literacytrust.org.uk

Interviews with popular authors abound on publishers' sites through which pupils can gain an appreciation of how writers work at their craft. Promotional activities on the web bring the authors' work to life, offer advice and promote writing in numerous ways.

The Internet offers pupils the opportunity to publish their writing and receive critical feedback from an audience. The published pages can be on the school intranet which is only visible from within the school, on the school website or through a site aimed at encouraging young writers.

▼ Suggested activities

- 'All about me': pupils submit a short account of themselves into a web-based form which places it alongside other pupils' submissions.
- Read some creative writing around a particular theme submitted by other children: www.kotn.ntu.ac.uk
- 'Now its your turn': pupils finish stories started by famous authors such as Jacqueline Wilson, or complete a poem by John Hegley: www.writehere.org.uk
- Write on a theme, e.g. pirate adventures: www.ukoln.ac.uk/services/treasure
- Read stories, review books and submit stories to the Young Writer Magazine: www.mystworld.com/youngwriter
- Write a story of exactly 100 words on the word 'curiously' for a writing competition. Use the automatic word-count facility

▼ Assessment focus

- Printed or published stories.

YEARS 5 / P6

28 Evaluating Sources: Newspapers ▼

Learning objectives ▼

Pupils:
- learn to critically evaluate a variety of different accounts of the same event;
- understand the difference between journalistic styles;
- understand the main features of newspapers including layout, range of information, voice, level of formality, etc.

ICT resources ▼

Internet access
Word processor with DTP features, e.g. columns and text wrap around images
Printer
Digital camera (optional)
Scanner (optional)

Vocabulary ▼

page layout
style
author/journalist
format
graphics
images
columns
headline
heading
import
text wrap

▼ Introduction

Websites are a very accessible source of comparative styles within a genre. On-line periodicals, newspapers and journals offer a free and current source of material for pupils to evaluate. Most major newspapers have their main headline articles instantly available on their website, e.g. *The Telegraph*.

Good word-processing packages allow pupils to create newspaper-style output using columns, and where text 'wraps' around the pictures.

A digital camera or scanner enables 'local' images to be produced to support the account.

▼ Suggested activities

This activity takes place inside and outside of the literacy hour with groups refining their 'article' over a period of time.

- Locate the reporting of a current event in three on-line newspapers. Groups prepare a short statement about the differences, e.g. factual differences; missing information; style of reporting; amount of text and how images are related to the text.
- Provide a headline and ask groups to write and illustrate an article in the style of a particular newspaper, e.g. '*Dog, bitten by postman, goes to court!*'
- Use a word processor or DTP program to create different text/image formats. (If the software enables 'saving as a web page' this enables pupils to view it in the same format as the original documents.)

▼ Assessment focus

- Observation of comments on different presentational styles.
- Completed writing frames on research into the different styles of newspapers.
- Printed report before formatting and final copy of newspaper article.

Learning objectives ▼

Pupils learn to:
- re-purpose text for use in different contexts;
- find and select information from a number of sources;
- produce explanatory text that illustrates clarity and conciseness;
- read, compare and evaluate arguments and discussions.

ICT resources ▼

Internet access
Content specific CD-ROMs or encyclopedia
Word processor
Printer (colour)
Presentation software such as *PowerPoint* (Microsoft)

Vocabulary ▼

Internet
key words
website
search engine
discussion group
image
DTP
author
text

▼ Introduction

Reference and context specific CD-ROMs and the Internet can provide text for pupils to manipulate. Text can be selected in a web page and then copied and pasted into a word processor, e.g. *Britannica* which is available on-line.

The 'Virtual library' website, www.thelib.org, is a useful way of tracking down on-line books on almost any subject. It can, however, produce a surfeit of American books.

Free text search engines, such as www.google.com or *Ask Jeeves for Kids*, produce a rich set of different types of resources on a particular topic. It is advisable to check the results of using particular key words before the session or even to 'suggest' an appropriate question that the teacher has already tried.

A writing frame can help pupils who need further support to be selective in the type of information they collect.

▼ Suggested activities

- Select text, from the Internet or CD-ROM, on a particular theme or topic and re-purpose it for another use, e.g. 'Should whales be killed for food?'.
- Take a successful product currently on the market and describe it in terms that the Patent Office could understand. Research the Patent Office website for the submission form for registering new inventions.
- Summarise a piece of text on one slide in *PowerPoint* using bullet points.
- The class create a series of Trivial Pursuit type cards or multiple-choice questions in the style of 'Millionaire' using the information from a data source.
- Make a 'Fact or Fiction' book around aspects of science, technology or geography.

▼ Assessment focus

- Printed copies of final 'products' attached to printed source material.

30 Poetry ▼

Learning objectives ▼

Pupils learn to:
- find information on well-known poets;
- write poems in the style of another poet;
- identify the features of a number of distinctive poets.

ICT resources ▼

Internet access
Web page
Word processor (with talking facility)
Scanner (optional)

Vocabulary ▼

sequence
enter
layout
wordlist
compose
clip art
illustration
scanner
font
point size
graphic
find-replace

▼ Introduction

Poetry is made to be shared. The Internet abounds with poetry sites, many specifically providing a forum for pupils to share their poems. Poets such as Roger Mcgough, Caribbean poets such as Derek Walcott, and the humorous American poet Ken Nesbitt amongst many other all have sites dedicated to their work, or maintain their own sites. Teachers or pupils can find information about the poet's work, submit poems and even join in a workshop, e.g. Work with Jack Perlutsky. Tip: Go into a web search engine, e.g. www.google.com, enter '*children poetry online*' to produce a list of most key sites. The Children's Poetry website has regular guest poets such as Brian Moses.

The Poetry Society is a national resource based at the Royal Festival Hall which has extensive resources for teachers and pupils. On-line try the 'lost quotation' feature or simply use the links to poetry sites.

▼ Suggested activities

- Remove rhyming words on alternate lines of a poem and replace them with others. Offer alternative rhyming words in a word grid.
- Browse and submit poems on one of the many poetry sites which publish children's work.
- Compile a class anthology of illustrated poems for the school website using a word processor that can generate web pages, e.g. *TextEase 2000*.
- Use a clicker grid to present pupils with lists of five and seven syllable words from which they create Haiku poems, e.g. grouped under seasons, nature and feelings.
- Compose a poem suitable for sending using a mobile phone text service. Use the conventions employed to economise on text entry.

▼ Assessment focus

- Completed poems printed out or published on the website.
- Pupils talk about the features of different poets.

Learning objectives ▼

Pupils learn:
- to read further stories by a familiar author;
- to consider how texts are rooted in the writer's experience;
- to describe and review their own reading habits and to widen their reading experience;
- how they and other readers respond to a variety of texts.

ICT resources ▼

Internet access
Word processor

Vocabulary ▼

author
website
review
rating
database
publisher

▼ Introduction

Reader development is a familiar concept to librarians. Answering the question "Do you have any more Horrid Henry books?" can lead pupils to new pastures in reading material. When pupils 'catch the bug' for a particular author, it can be the motivation to become an avid reader. To maintain the motivation and move the reader on to similar or new types of books is an important skill for the teacher. An intimate knowledge of children's books helps, but there are new web-based resources that teachers and pupils can use.

Public library initiatives such as 'Branching Out' offer reader development resources for all ages. The Booktrust on Booktrusted.com is a site 'for all those concerned with what children read'.

▼ Suggested activities

- Pupils select their favourite book and then locate the book on one of the websites and download as many reviews as they feel appropriate. Use the reviews to construct a table of criteria that pupils use in describing preferences for particular books. Describe its characteristics in terms of genre, character appeal, settings, descriptive language, etc.
- Use an on-line bookshop to review all the books available by a particular author, e.g. Anne Fine.
- Use reader development sites, e.g. Branching Out to allow pupils to find books which build on their current reading.
- Use the websites to select a book as a present for a friend or relative whose book preferences they have investigated.
- Use a safe search engine, such as www.AskJeevesforKids.com and www.Yahooligans.com, to find books in a particular genre, e.g. humorous, fantasy.

▼ Assessment focus

- Printed or written reviews.
- Suggestions for further reading.
- Understanding of criteria people use to express opinions on books.

Learning objectives ▼

Pupils learn to:
- express their ideas about a story or poem;
- be aware of authors and discuss preferences and reasons for these;
- write a book review for a specified audience based on evaluations of plot, character and language;
- write discursively about a novel or story.

ICT resources ▼

Access to the Internet on one or more computers
Word processor
Printer

Vocabulary ▼

website
Internet
submit

▼ Introduction

Large book retailers offer readers the opportunity to read professional reviews and to see the reaction of other readers. Large on-line bookshops all welcome comments on the books they are featuring on the website.

A partnership of libraries around the country has generated a set of interactive resources to be used by teachers and pupils during KS2 English lessons. The site is called 'Stories from the Web': www.storiesfromtheweb.org

The aim of the site is to support reader development by allowing pupils to read more and share their views on books and poems they have read. The project aims to track the developing relationship between the use of public libraries and reader development activity. Activities on the site include: reading and writing stories; reading and submitting reviews; interviews with authors; writing to authors; submitting poems, rhymes and limericks.

▼ Suggested activities

- Visit an on-line bookshop's children's site and download some reviews written by children about books the class are familiar with.
- Pupils read a chosen book from the site and write a review on paper. The review can be transferred to a word processor and finally to the school website, for others to read.
- Use a writing frame to structure pupils' reviews.

▼ Assessment focus

Pupils:
- print out word-processed reviews or website submissions;
- do a verbal account of reading a book.

Learning objectives ▼

Pupils learn:
- to read further stories by a familiar author;
- to describe and review their own reading habits and to widen their reading experience;
- to express their own views.

ICT resources ▼

Internet access
E-mail

Vocabulary ▼

Internet
website
discussion group
e-mail
author
edit

▼ Introduction

The Library Association (LA) is the professional body for librarians/information professionals from all fields. Carnegie Shadowing is one of the activities that they support for schools. The Carnegie Medal is awarded each year for 'outstanding writing in a children's book'. It was first won by Arthur Ransome in 1936. Over 10,000 children each year take part in the 'shadowing' process which parallels the judging process. Reading groups take on the process of reading and reviewing the books against the same criteria used by the judges.

There is a tight timescale between the shortlisted books being announced and the final date when the winner is announced by the LA. Pupils can then decide how wrong the judges were. A comment from a teacher: 'This is my fourth year of shadowing and it's a very rewarding experience, there is eager competition to be chosen to join the group.' The Library Association website is at www.la-hq.org.uk

▼ Suggested activities

- Year 5–6 / P6–7 pupils shortlist books for KS1 pupils.
- Year 6 / P7 pupils work with the local secondary school library on younger Carnegie titles.
- Write a book review of exactly fifty words. (In MS Word use the File>Properties>Statistics feature to check the word count).
- Hold a series of Carnegie lunches (sandwiches!) in the school library/resources area to discuss reading progress.
- Use the Library Association website for exchanging opinions, information and reviews of the shortlisted titles.
- Link with other schools via e-mail and share shortlists.
- Post the reviews of the most favoured books on the school website.

▼ Assessment focus

- Monitor the number of books read by pupils.
- Pupils print out their reviews for the teacher to assess.
- Monitor the quality of discussions within groups as they exchange ideas.

34 Creating a Website ▼

Pupils learn:
- how to bring work to a published form;
- to identify features of non-fiction texts such as headings, bullet points, etc.
- to use ICT to plan and revise writing to improve accuracy, layout and presentation.

ICT resources ▼

TextEase 2000 (Softease Ltd) or *Word 2000*
or
Web authoring programme such as *Hotdog Junior* (RM) or *Dreamweaver* (Macromedia)
Digital camera
Links to websites of graphical tools such as buttons and clip art (optional)
Scanner

Vocabulary ▼

web authoring software
multimedia
navigation
digital image
page format
HTML
point size
template
graphic
Intranet
Internet
links
publishing

▼ Introduction

Many word processors, such as *Word 2000* or *TextEase 2000*, have the facility to save the work in a web format making creating pages for the Internet a relatively straightforward process. Pupils can work in a familiar context of the word processor and finally view their work using a web browser such as Internet Explorer. The page(s) can be stored locally and viewed by the class, or by the rest of the school on the school intranet. For quality work, the school may decide to feature some pages on the school website.

Specialist web authoring software, e.g. *Hotdog Junior* or *Dreamweaver* have additional features which help manage the structure of a website and provide custom-made navigation features that link pages together.

Pupils' illustrations, done using conventional drawing tools, can be incorporated in the page by scanning them and using them in a graphic file format. Pictures from a digital camera can be incorporated and text added.

▼ Suggested activities

- Access a selected list of school websites and compile a report on the types of pages they have made available, e.g. the BECTa website awards.
- Research local history sources at the public library and create a series of web pages to feature on the school website.
- Using a template, each pupil creates a page featuring a picture and information about themselves. (For safety reasons these should only be made available internally).
- Create an anthology of poetry written and illustrated by the pupils.
- All classes collaborate to provide a view of the school for the school website.

▼ Assessment focus

- Printed contributions to published web pages.
- Content, design and organisation of materials produced.

Learning objectives ▼

Pupils learn to:
- communicate ideas which would be difficult if only text were used;
- examine the needs of a target audience;
- collaborate with others to write stories, planning for a particular audience;
- write non-chronological reports linked to other subjects.

ICT resources ▼

Hyperstudio (TAG) or similar authoring software such as *TextEase 2000* (Softease Ltd), *TextEase Studio* (Softease Ltd)
Word-processing software with ability to import graphics
Scanner
Web browser (optional)

Vocabulary ▼

multimedia
image
menu
icons
hyperlink
buttons
sound samples
graphic
animation
sound
sample
attach

▼ Introduction

Multimedia authoring software, e.g. *Hyperstudio, Illuminatus* or *TextEase 2000* allows pupils to construct exciting pages, to explore linking text graphics sounds and video to produce an interactive presentation. The banks of resources such as sounds, buttons and clip art enable pupils at KS1/P1-3 to create their own resources with a simple suite of tools.

Pupils start by creating a series of 'screens' with appropriate text and images and then begin to 'hyperlink' them together with buttons created using a tool kit that allows any item or area of the screen to become a link to sound, video or another screen. Animation, graphics and multimedia effects such as sounds can be added to the slides.

▼ Suggested activities

- Create a talking book for younger pupils based on one of their set texts. Animate some key words on each page to introduce ideas such as verbs.
- Create a talking book using a 'talking word processor' such as *Granada Writer*. Using multimedia authoring software, e.g. *Hyperstudio* pupils can read the words (sentences) and record them to use in the presentation.
- Present the different musical instruments in an orchestra, with sound sampled from a recording or directly through a microphone.
- Present local history alongside scanned photographs or pictures from a digital camera. Pupils or local people read the words which can be heard by clicking on the text.

▼ Assessment focus

- Quality of talking book in terms of content, interactivity, navigation, graphics and their suitability for the intended audience.
- The persuasive, motivating or informative nature of the text content.
- The clarity of the argument or report or information.

Learning objectives ▼

Pupils learn to:
- write alternative endings for a known story;
- use different ways of planning stories;
- collaborate with others to write chapters or stories using a plan.

ICT resources ▼

Word processor supporting hypertext such as *MS PowerPoint, TextEase 2000* or a multimedia authoring package such as *Hyperstudio* (TAG)
Access to the Internet on one or more computers (optional)
Multimedia authoring software

Vocabulary ▼

hyperlink
links
sequence
multimedia
image
template
slide
website
Internet

▼ Introduction

Many pupils will be familiar with books which invite the reader to choose their own route through a story and so create alternative stories each time the book is read. Word-processing software which can make active links from within a page of text to other pages or images can be used to produce 'interactive' stories. The active links are often referred to as hyperlinks. Links can bring up text, images, sound and graphics. The stories can be viewed as text documents or saved as a web page which can be viewed in a web browser, e.g. Internet Explorer or Netscape.

Each link on the page must follow logically through to the next. For example, explore some stories on: www.trace.ntu.ac.uk/hypertext

▼ Suggested activities

- Create an example text of a familiar story, e.g. Little Red Riding Hood as a series of linked pages.
- Each group generates alternative 'next steps' at each decision point.
- Provide the initial opening of the story (available from *Magic Pen Starters Page*) and pupils provide alternatives at choice points.
- Collaborate with other schools using e-mail to compile an interactive story which is then placed on the respective schools' websites.

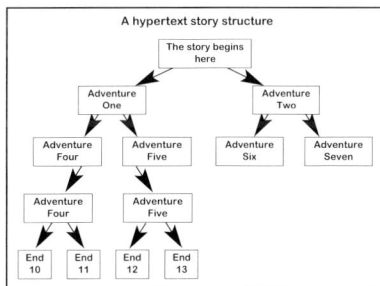

A hypertext story structure

▼ Assessment focus

- Track individual's ideas by identifier on each page and observation of discussion within groups.

Learning objectives ▼

Pupils learn to:
- use language appropriate to find and select information from a number of sources;
- identify and use the main features associated with persuasive text;
- investigate how style and vocabulary are used to convince the reader.

ICT resources ▼

Content specific CD-ROM reference materials or electronic encyclopedia
Internet access to reference material (optional)
DTP software, such as
MS Publisher (Microsoft) (optional)
Web-authoring software (optional)

Vocabulary ▼

cut and paste
layout
compose
clip art
graphic
illustration
scanner
font
point size
graphic

▼ Introduction

The Internet can provide a rich source of persuasive texts on almost any subject. Politics, advertising, religious groups, pressure groups, manufacturers and newspapers are potential areas to explore.

MS Publisher offers a range of templates to create flyers, folded leaflets, posters and magazines into which pupils can write or paste text from a word processor and pictures from the Internet, scanner or digital camera. Wizards offer the user a chance to customise the templates. Many word processors offer a range of templates or formats, e.g. *TextEase 2000* offers a poster format for printer output and *MS Word* has a number of templates for different purposes if they are installed on the network or classroom PC.

▼ Suggested activities

- Pupils examine printed materials from a variety of sources as examples of persuasive texts, e.g. leaflets, posters, flyers, magazines, newspapers.
- Select text from the Internet or CD-ROM, on a particular theme or topic and re-purpose it for another use, e.g. 'Should whales be killed for food?'.
- Groups prepare a *PowerPoint* presentation containing five slides that argue a particular point of view. The class judge the effectiveness of each presentation given to them using the slides.
- Produce a bi-fold leaflet to advertise a local amenity such as the library, museum or sports centre.
- Produce a web page that outlines the case for protecting an animal or environment.

▼ Assessment focus

- Observation of individual contribution to group work.
- Quality of products in terms of objectives and audience:
  - *PowerPoint* presentation;
  - web page;
  - printed materials.

📖 YEAR 6 / P7

Glossary ▼

address	the unique electronic location to which e-mail can be sent
address book	a piece of software which stores e-mail addresses on a computer in the same way as a normal address book
animation	the process of drawing separate images, each one modified slightly and displayed in sequence to create the impression of motion
attachment	a computer file attached to an e-mail
bold	used to describe text which has been made bold and appears darker with thicker lines
browser	computer software used for viewing web pages
CD-ROM	Compact Disc Read-Only Memory – used for storing large amounts of computer files
cells	the boxes within a spreadsheet or table
clip art	illustrations and icons used within desktop publishing programs
columns	term used in desktop publishing and word-processing to describe text organised into vertical columns
commands	any direct instruction to the computer, usually typed in control programs; a computer will only understand a limited number of commands
compose	used to describe writing an e-mail within an e-mail program
concept keyboard	(overlay keyboard) – a touch sensitive keypad which can have paper overlays placed over the keys
cursor	a visual reference point for the user showing them where their actions will occur
cut and paste	text or images can be removed from one program to be placed or 'pasted' in another; the text or image is placed in a temporary storage area, the clipboard, when it is cut from a program
data	numbers, characters or images entered and stored on a computer
data entry box	an area of the screen which allows the user to enter data
data projector	used for displaying a large copy of the computer screen on a wall or screen, especially useful for presentations, and teaching
database	one or more large structured sets of data, usually associated with software used to update and query the data
delete	removing information from a computer file
desktop publishing	creation of a publication format on a personal computer; this can contain text, graphics and images
digital camera	similar to a conventional camera this captures images in a digital format instead of on film, ready for use with a computer
discussion group	a web page where people discuss topics by sending messages to the group
disk	a small, portable plastic disc, used for storing and transporting computer files
drag-drop	on a computer a drag and drop interface is one which allows you to drag items around the screen using the mouse; these items can be dropped anywhere by releasing the mouse button
edit	changing the contents of a document
e-mail	messages, usually text, sent from one person to another via computer; can be sent automatically to a large mailing list
export	converting a computer file into a format which is readable by another computer program
file	any piece of information stored on a computer has to be stored in a file
find-replace	an automated search of text in a document which literally finds a set word or sentence and replaces it with another
font	a style of typeface

form	part of a web page used to collect information from the user
graphic	an image or artwork used on a computer
grid	a set of equally spaced, parallel, vertical and horizontal lines used for laying out a document or illustration
hard disk	the storage area inside the computer where files are saved
Html	Hyper Text Markup Language – a tag-based language used to define the style, layout and content within a web page
image format	images stored on computer are stored in different formats depending on what they are being used for
import	converting a computer file format from one not normally supported by the program
inbox	the area in the e-mail program where e-mails which have been received are stored
insert	usually referring to the act of inserting a piece of information from an external source into the current file which is being edited
interactive	term used to describe a program where the user is involved in entering information and receiving feedback as a continual process
interactive whiteboard	an interactive whiteboard can be linked to a computer so that drawing on the board executes commands in a similar way to using a mouse on the screen
Internet	the worldwide collection of inter-connected computer networks that all communicate in the same language
intranet	a private network of web pages where access is restricted to people within a company or organisation; information on an Intranet can only be accessed by people who have been granted permission
key word	a word or words which might be used to search for a website or data within a database
keyboard	a device consisting of a number of mechanical buttons (keys) which the user presses to input characters into a computer
links	a link will transport you from one Internet site to another with just a click of your mouse; links can be text or graphic; text links will usually be underlined and often in a different colour; a graphic link will usually have a coloured frame around it
load	something is loaded when it is transferred from storage into the computer's memory and is executed
log on	the entering of a user name and password in order to access information on a computer
memory	the electronic storage area used in a computer; information stored in memory is only stored temporarily
monitor	the screen which displays the information from the computer
mouse	device used to move an arrow or pointer around the screen in order to select various command options from the menu bar
multimedia	human computer interaction involving text, graphics, voice and video; the term is often associated with CD-ROM software
navigation	the menu or system used for finding things within a website
net	short for Internet
on-line	a computer which is actively connected to the Internet is considered on-line; often people will say they are on-line meaning they have access to the Internet and have an e-mail address, but may not necessarily be connected to the internet at that moment
page layout	the design and style of a document
point size	used to define how large the user wishes a font to appear

pointer	the cursor which appears on the computer screen and is controlled by either the mouse or keyboard
presentation software	a software tool designed to make computer-based presentations or OHTs
program	a series of instructions that tell a computer what to do
record	an entry within a database, about a person, place, event or some other item
save	a file is copied from the computer's memory to disc or some other form of storage
scanner	used for converting images from photographs and other printed documents into digital pictures or text on a computer
search engine	tool available on the Internet which allows you to search by key words for information on the Internet
sensor	an electronic device used to measure a physical quantity, usually to provide data for a computer
shift	the shift key is used to type characters from the keyboard which are shown above the normal character for that key; the shift key must be held down in combination with another key
slide show	a selection of picture and/or text slides, presented one after another
spell checker	a tool used to check the spelling on a document
symbol	any character which is not punctuation, a letter in the alphabet or a number
table	a collection of information organised into corresponding columns and rows
templates	a document into which a user can enter information without having to define the rest of the document
text box	area in a word processor where a user can enter text
text wrap	causes text to automatically go on to the next line of a document if it reaches the end of the previous line (often used to describe the flow of text around a picture)
thesaurus	most word processors contain a thesaurus, providing an easy way to find words with similar meanings
toolbar	usually at the top of the program, the toolbar contains all the most commonly used options from the program's menu system; each option is usually depicted as an icon
tools	most programs provide a selection of tools; the tools are usually common but complex tasks which are made easier by the use of the tool
underline	causes everything which is typed to be <u>underlined</u>
undo	most programs remember what you have been doing, and selecting undo will literally undo the last thing you did
URL	Uniform Resource Locator – the unique address which is typed into a web browser to access a specific web page
view	the user can control the size and layout of information on the screen, e.g. View whole page
website	a selection of documents on the world wide web which are linked together
word bank	a feature of some word-processing packages that offers the user a set (bank) of words that can be selected and pasted into a document
word processor	a program used for creating documents including letters, books and reports
world wide web	the system of computers around the world used for exchange of information on the Internet; every computer which is providing information for viewing on web pages is part of the world wide web

Index ▼

Acknowledgements

The author and publishers would like to thank the following people:
Phil Quinn, Jo Westbrook, Mike Blamires, Andrew Lambirth, Georgina Stein,
Kathy Gooch, Canterbury Christ Church University College, KITSch (Kent IT in
Schools Programme).
Screen shots: *Sherlock* (Topologika Software); *Stories from the Web* (Stories from
the Web); *Phonics* (BBC Education); *Powerpoint* (reprinted by permission from
Microsoft Corporation).

Every effort has been made to trace the copyright holders, but if any have been
inadvertently overlooked the publishers will be pleased to make the necessary
arrangements at the first opportunity.